7.25

P9-AFF-724

WITHDRAWN

JUL 01 2024

DAVID O. McKAY LIBRARY
BYU-IDAHO

Essay Index

FOND OPINIONS

by

STEPHEN GWYNN

KENNIKAT PRESS
Port Washington, N. Y./London

Essay Index

FOND OPINIONS

First published in 1938
Reissued in 1971 by Kennikat Press
Library of Congress Catalog Card No: 70-122877
ISBN 0-8046-1334-6

Manufactured by Taylor Publishing Company   Dallas, Texas

ESSAY AND GENERAL LITERATURE INDEX REPRINT SERIES

Most fond and winnowed opinions.

HAMLET.

Hath there been such a time—I'd fain know that—
That I have positively said, "'Tis so",
And it proved otherwise?

POLONIUS.

To E. A. M. T.

THESE essays were mostly written many years before I asked leave to set your initials here. But since they were largely about agreeable virtues, it seemed impossible to offer such a collection to you while it said nothing about hospitality; so one more has been added: I wish it were worthier of its occasion.

May I say this too? Having run uncountable times for help to the Dictionary of National Biography, and knowing what all men of letters owe to the generous enterprise of its publisher, I take my opportunity of acknowledging that debt in a book which is dedicated to his daughter.

February, 1938.   S. G.

MOST of what will be found here appeared a considerable time ago, by Lady Rhondda's surprising indulgence, in *Time and Tide*. "Happiness" was published, not less surprisingly, in *Blackwood's Magazine*: "The Habit of Beauty" in *The Times*, and "On being Shocked" in *The Spectator*. I have to thank my editors, first for publishing and now for allowing me to reprint in a revised form. For these opinions, since they were first aired, have been, in Hamlet's phrase, "winnowed".

STEPHEN GWYNN

CONTENTS

HAPPINESS

HAPPINESS is a big word, so big that one is shy of writing about it—as if it were Love or Life; and, indeed, it is the flower of both. Yet every poet, great or small, thinks it the most natural thing in the world to write about Love or Life, and why should prose be shamefaced?

Happiness, perhaps, lies nearer the domain of prose and the meaning of it was anatomised, macerated, and reduced to, on the whole, a satisfactory formula more than two thousand years ago. "The working of man's spirit according to its own excellence in a complete period of life": that is a rendering of the definition which Aristotle reached after many terse pages. Yet for all Aristotle's labour, and that of his successors, who knows, or knowing it can impart, the secret of happiness?

A thousand volumes prove that it is a pleasure to write of our favourite pursuits: such writers at times create an echo of their own delight, a shadowy enjoyment which others can be made to share—but only on a condition: their readers must have known the thrill. But it is a wise man that knows his own happiness, and some happy nature, reading this or some such essay, might on reflection realise where his happiness lies; conceivably even, in a strange world, might for the first time discover that he is happy.

Happiness dwells on the borderland where work passes into play. Somebody said that a man is never completely himself but when he is playing; it is no less true that he is never happy unless he is completely himself. That is why happiness is so big a word; it involves the whole nature.

None denies the difference, and the value of that difference, between a good painter's picture and another's reproduction of it. Yet what exactly is lost in the reproduction? I think, the happiness which a sensitive copyist may feel, but can never recreate. Even the artist himself can hardly live over again that piece of his own vitality.

But for us all there is the business of living. One can hardly overstress the importance of work to happiness, which assuredly will not come of doing nothing: if you lie inert, you are a lump, and probably a complaining lump.

But if you are happy, there is no need to prove that you are not a cumberer of the ground. Happiness is its own justification, and the test whether it be truly happiness is easy: does it reflect itself? You can shut yourself up with a pleasure like a schoolboy with a pot of jam, but no one can monopolise or isolate happiness; people come to it as to a fire in winter. There are rich and, as the phrase goes, idle men who make happiness about them by their mere being.

Happiness, unlike pleasure, is giving, not taking. Work is service; and to live so that you render service by merely living is perhaps the most difficult work of all.

Sometimes indeed happiness seems to walk in a garden like a child among flowers. Yet the child who in a garden finds real happiness is the child who can live with flowers, delighting in their life—not the greedy little human for whom flowers only satisfy the instinct of acquisition; they are picked, they wither, and soon the moment's pleasure is done. It is true that any child may be happy in gathering a posy for one it loves, but here the child is not self-sufficing in its garden. It is like most of us, who never alone enjoy to the full any beauty of sound, form, or

3

colour, but must always be picturing to ourselves another's delight which, sharing with us, would more than double our own.

Modern sentimentality inclines to rate that childish early happiness as the most complete of all, because it is so independent of externals that it seems happiness unmixed, undisturbed by any thought of work doing or to be done. Yet since the child has properly no function but to live and grow, if it grows well it is doing its work; and without some enveloping love in the background to which its being can respond, no child grows well. At the root of its solitary happiness there is communion.

Yet, though happiness cannot be lonely, it must know how to be alone. The bulk of our work may not be done in solitude, but the best of it must always be done there. For what really expresses the man he must plunge into himself. You cannot delegate the work in which happiness resides.

Yet that energy may express itself in the power of delegation. A man who loves the work of giving others work that they can love is happy in creating opportunities for happiness; and in some ways that is the ideal energy. Still, its happiness is precarious, because in the rush and hurry of many relations, a man

4

has difficulty to call his soul his own. Happiness is often shown in a crowd, but very seldom found there.

The artist is safer, because his work is no less than to reproduce and communicate his own happiness: he offers us not the seed but the flower; we seek from him the expression of his secret felicity. Old Turner was on the surface a disagreeable brute, yet he must have known heaven upon earth, for he has shown us his vision of it. To communicate the thrill —that is not to be a *marchand de bonheur*, purveyor of good luck, but a dealer in the very stuff of happiness.

For a certain period in Europe there was a literary affectation of unhappiness. Byron was its great man: and in spite of his fopperies, Byron was much too great to have seriously undervalued happiness. The men to whom he was attracted were happy men, healthy natures—notably Walter Scott, who returned his liking; but the one of all others for whom Byron had real affection was Tom Moore. If Moore had genius at all, it was a genius for happiness; his literature was little more than an extension of his personal charm. He was understood because he was happy, happy because he was understood.

And yet I think that Byron, who distorted
and falsified all understanding of his utterance, and even the utterance itself, by his
wilful pose of unhappiness, achieved in the
end a happiness higher than Moore ever knew.
From a literature which he himself had tainted
with insincerity, he escaped into the sincerity
of action; and his last lyric has what can
scarcely be discovered elsewhere in his work
—the ring of a happy heart. "Awake—not
Greece, she is awake"; no unhappy man wrote
that. He began to live when, instead of talking about dying, he found something worth
dying for.

The radical vice of Byronism, which spread
all over Europe like a disease, was that it
represented unhappiness as a mark of distinction, as if happiness were something
vulgar and superficial. That is a whimpering
doctrine. Happiness is a difficult thing to
achieve, and it is the business of us all to
strive after it, for it is the evidence that we
are doing our work well. The Byronic hero
never had any work; he and work were
strangers; his whole time was given up to
creating unhappiness, and contemplating what
he had created.

There are some who think themselves less

than happy because they do not again achieve the height of felicity which they have once known. Stevenson was an admirable moralist, and never used words loosely, but he wrote from Samoa to his friend: "Happy! I was only happy once, that time at Hyères." This that he thinks of is not happiness; it is momentary by its nature, it takes indeed two natures to make it; it is enchantment, it is festival, when work stops and all the faculties swim in the delight of being. It may irradiate long spaces of life with an afterglow, it may transform the relation out of which it springs; but it cannot be lasting, for while it lasts, nothing else is contemplated.

To speak of such a state as the only happiness is merely twisting round the French saying about *les beaux jours quand nous étions si malheureux.* They were *beaux jours* because we had the capacity then to be so radiant; life was a brilliant succession of ups and downs, life was youth, in short. This extreme felicity, or that extreme despair, belongs to youth, and while either state comes back, youth is not ended. Still, sooner or later, youth ends; but there is no time limit for happiness.

Perhaps it is even more difficult to be

7

happy when one is young; Aristotle quotes with assent a verse that was old two thousand years ago: "But sweetest of all it is to attain the end of desire." Youth never clearly knows its own desire—it wants so many things; it has not found out wherein its soul's best energy lies. Moreover, happiness, though it cannot be felt at all moments, is a state, not a flash: a man can hardly claim it before he has got fairly into his stride.

Someone in a novel of Maupassant's says that the best years of life are those between fifty and sixty, when your position is made and you are not too old to enjoy it. That is to look at things rather from the standpoint of pleasure only; but in another sense it is often true, at all events for a man. Power comes then, and power is certainly not necessary to happiness, but it means the consummation of a life's energy. Failure to achieve power, for one whose work aims at it, does not condemn to unhappiness. His soul is not the slave of failure; yet what happiness he may be said to have, flowers on an unkindly soil. In the best of work, at the best of happiness, no limiting resistance is felt; the nature gives all that is in it; there may be a weight on the shoulders, yet it does not

8

gall or hamper. But worry is the negation of happiness, for it means a distraction of energy, so that your heart cannot be fully in what you crave to do.

The world knows many instances where men and women have successfully broken out of a sphere of life or work in which they felt unhappy, and burst through into one where they could be happily themselves. Most of us can add a long list of cases where the attempt to make this transference has ended in disappointment or disaster. Still, it seemed to me the other day large wisdom when a father consented ungrudgingly that his son should abandon prosperous chances in a bank for the pursuit of art; all the larger wisdom because success in art did not seem probable. But there was one more radiant face in the Latin quarter of Paris.

The war taught us elders to revise our values, and to determine that such young lives as were spared should not be stinted of their vitality. We had let them face so many risks for an uncommercial honour that we were less ready to forbid a throw for some uninsurable happiness.

You will seldom get happiness by going to look for it. It does not exist in the abstract;

there must be a vehicle, a medium, to embody it. The higher your conscious aim, perhaps the less likely is happiness; assuredly, the more concrete your big aim, the less possible it is of achievement so complete that happiness can result.

Yet there may be happiness behind the strained and tormented face of one pursuing with formidable energy his dream or his quest; if there is this aura, you will find that others count it a happiness to share in that energy, to be in communion with that spirit.

There is no such need of proof when some gentle modest happiness falls into its un-assuming place in the natural scheme of things. Physical well-being is a kind of it; an unselfish person who has good health gives daily of his strength, or of hers. Serenity goes with such health, and serenity is a great part of happiness; it is what makes nuns' happy faces. Perhaps because they have shut off from their lives great fields of energy, serenity comes easier to them, and perhaps happiness, with limitations, is more attainable.

But to reach Aristotle's full standard, happiness must live in the world, it must be in touch with the vital currents of delight;

and it comes best of all when it is the answer to long desire, the reward of long labour. Some lives after release from the war made a fragrance, they were so happy. My type of the happy man will be always a soldier friend who returned at the end of thirty years' soldiering to the home where he was reared, and fell to working the acres which his father had owned. Everything about Michael was agreeable—house and land and sport and neighbours; he had an active, handsome body, good brains to work with—excellent material for happiness to grow from, but in no sense exceptional; yet from it he made something unique. We knew why after his death, for we recognised then that we had known no other man so unselfish.

In Michael, thought for others had become second nature, so that in every kind act he always seemed to be doing what he liked best.

Every happiness, like every vice, is marked not only with a personal accent but with the accents of a country. There is nothing pleasanter to meet than a well-married couple in France; they have a talent for sharing each other's life, and the man's work, instead of being, as often happens elsewhere, a barrier between their lives, is the very substance of their bond. Balzac knew this when he described César Birotteau's pride in his work and in his wife, and beside it, his wife's pride in César's work. That is what makes the household of this merchant of soaps and hair-restorers so intimately and characteristically French; for nothing, not even their laughter, can be so expressive of a people as their happiness.

Since happiness spreads and enhances itself by reflection, happy people are much happier together. And another's presence may be the essential for happiness, which therefore can be made with small expense, yet is often the hardest thing in the world to come by. Denial of a desired companionship is not the easiest privation to bear. Yet, if real happiness be on that condition really attainable, then the pain of privation is happiness at one remove; happiness that may in a moment pass from latency into radiance.

And where there is radiance there may also surely be obscuration. There is ebb and flow in every happiness, it varies like the earth.

On the other hand, since there is ebb and flow, the power of being happy must wax and wane; and perhaps where there is the finest gift for happiness, there is also most feeling of its defeat. No created thing can look so miserable as a caged singing-bird, and one may see the happy utterly depressed, craving for the echo of their own singing in the life of others.

There is no luxury so great as the luxury of dispensing happiness, and if some physical lassitude checks the vitality, damps the flame, then the ebb may reach down to despondency.

Yet human instinct gives the go-by to those who at the best are content, or not discontented; it cleaves to the happy, and perhaps most of all, to those who can only be happy at times; for the companion is always tempted with a hope that it may be his happiness, or hers, to call into play the latent power, until wakening it gives back a hundredfold the joy of living.

But how shifting and various the word is! for no two happinesses are the same.

Perhaps the highest happiness of all is merely the intense perception of living in a world of living beauty. Yet, is there high or low in this matter?

For some, happiness lies in the pursuit of

one great quest which leaves the pursuer indifferent to most of creation; for some again, happiness is made up of a number of little things, like life itself.

For some, it lies in a work, which, great or little, satisfies the doer; for others, happiness is sought as the condition without which their work cannot be done. If they are unhappy, as sometimes befalls, it is because privation checks their energy; they are like flowers which know that they blossom only in the sun. They are like the girl who craves instinctively for means to make herself as pretty as she can be.

Aristotle did not expect people to be happy on sixpence a day; he assumed that they had what they needed—he assumed even a certain splendour. One of the best treatises on happiness ever written is the "Charwoman's Daughter", and James Stephens does not deny himself and us the satisfaction of bestowing splendour in the last page upon his Mary Make-believe. But the last page merely transplants her gift for happiness out of a Dublin slum into a kindly Irish garden.

The war which drove ugly flashlights into the recesses of human nature revealed also much of happiness, when half the happinesses

14

in Europe were held in suspense. That time
of meetings and partings gave experience of
the renewal of love, without the bitter fore-
taste of anger. And many, I think, achieved
happiness in determining that a parting should
not be unhappy.

Whether in war or peace, serenity is perhaps the hardest part of happiness to master.
Age is believed to possess it by a compensating bounty of nature, yet I think it comes
easier to youth. Youth trusts itself, and is
confident it will never do anyone a bad turn.
To doubt yourself in essentials, as age inclines
to do, is to be unhappy; for the happy heart
cannot be self-tormenting.

It is curious to look through literature and
think of the happy people one has known in
print. Is there anybody happy in Thackeray's
work? in Thomas Hardy's? for that matter,
in Meredith's? In Thackeray, I can only think
of Colonel Newcome and possibly Major
Dobbin; Thackeray it is plain, knew some
one individual in whom he felt that unselfish-
ness and chivalry stood out like beacons in
a deservedly unhappy world. Hardy can show
you people who have the gift for happiness,
he can make you feel that in happier circumstances they might have been happy—

like his Tess. Meredith does the same with his Lucy Feverel; I think he leads one to believe that Clara Middleton will be happy and will give happiness, though that stage of her being is not shown. But Beauchamp is a happy nature and so is Vittoria; they have its radiant strength. Dickens, now, had the feeling for happiness—it is part of his prodigious vitality. Charles Reade had it—look at his little masterpiece "Peg Woffington" for instance; and Trollope, in his plain substantial way, could give you a happy atmosphere, as definite as the smell of plum-pudding and as satisfying; and he could give you precisely the corresponding unhappiness.

Scott is so good to be with, you can understand why animals ran after him, and why the Dandie Dinmonts and other simple folk worshipped 'the Shirra'. Yet Scott has other spells to work with; but if you take from Goldsmith his happiness, all goes with it; his happiness is his wisdom, his wit and the gentle caress of his style; it is the essential quality of them all. Set him beside his greatest contemporary, the so reputed philosopher, and how does Johnson compare? Neither man was fortunate, as the common tests go; each of the two was covered with blemishes; but they stand out, Johnson with the memory of kind things done compensating unkind things said, and everywhere about him a sense of unmeasured delight in his own trampling powers: Goldsmith, a simple figure, comical enough, but carrying in his hand the image of happiness which he had wrought in squalor and misery out of such materials as long unhappy chance offered to his observation.

Of the poets, Wordsworth at his best gives the most of a serene happiness. Shélley has in its excess the temperament of extremes; happiness to him is always something precarious, not, as with Wordsworth, the strong well-rooted growth of the whole nature. Shakespeare here, as everywhere, runs the whole gamut; but nothing else in all literature has so exquisite a happiness as his pictures of girlhood, his Miranda and his Perdita. No one questions his serenity; for my part I do not think that any of the plays, except perhaps "Measure for Measure" and "Troilus and Cressida", was written by an unhappy soul. In the last distilment of their essence there is no bitterness: not even in "Lear". But who could say that Milton was happy, except as a quite young man? There is in him a satisfaction at seeing people damned, which would be inconceivable in Shakespeare and is incompatible with happiness. And look at his picture of Eden: where in all that fine writing is there even a suggestion of the happy heart?

For the simple quality of happiness, nothing else in literature can touch folk-song; just because it is so impersonal, the joy of living felt by the race. It may be melancholy in aspect—it often is; but you can enjoy being melancholy, like Jaques. Nobody can enjoy being unhappy.

Away out beyond folk lyric, lies the unearthly happiness of bird-song. There may be a greater volume of joy in the lark's music, and one aspect of happiness at least is the faculty of joy; but for choice, give me the wren: his note is so courageous, he has such confidence on a cold March afternoon that spring is at the door.

For, after all, if over the living globe "the towering shade advances", so also does the illimitable light. It is true we are between two darks, but does that dash the courage of the wren's song? And if we, who by our nature look before and after, who see dark ahead as well as behind, what then? We have our day, our chance of happiness in work; some day we shall have had it, but the work goes on and the cause. What is the cause?

Beauty, truth, goodness, justice—it has many names, and happiness is one of them.

It is assuredly not possible to be happy and think that the cause is losing and bound to lose all the time. Those who think that, lack the talent for happiness; yet perhaps compensation may be found for some among them —as for A. E. Housman, who at least must have known for certain hours the happiness of his flute-player, for he heard his tune come out clear and mellow, and heard us praise the tune.

But to imply, as he seems to, that you must be miserable unless you can be sure of going on for ever and ever—that, I confess, defeats me. Assuredly the happy should have enough gust for life to be willing to begin over again; I am as brave as that myself; but not for eternity, I thank you. Not without making my conditions; there is too much pitfall and gin to be picking one's way through for more than a few decades. Michael, indeed, used to say he would like to live to be a hundred, and I believed him; but then he was perfectly unselfish, and had an ador-

able stretch of salmon river. And perhaps—
but no, I would have backed him to be happy
while life lasted, even to a hundred. Is there
a better praise?

Aristotle refused to go into the question
whether people could be supposed to be
happy after they were dead. But he knew
and laid down that while they were alive,
their main end in life was to be happy, and
to remain happy, even though life should try
to get the better of them. There was a fine
fortitude about his conception of this excellence; I like a courageous happiness. Physical
courage allied to happiness is superb and
makes its own atmosphere, dispersing misery
and turning the balance, where it wavers
for so many, between collapse and resistance.

Yet finer infinitely than any physical courage is the courage of those hearts who, having
in them a beautiful capacity for happiness,
find it again and again smothered by ugly
chances, and who yet, when the sky clears
even a little, break out into the wren's song.

EXPERIENCE

STATISTICS never give what is really worth knowing, because they never can give it; the important facts are moral facts, and can only be ascertained by experience, which varies for each person.

There is, however, an experience of the race, having its expression in custom and manners, guides more elastic and adaptable than law, which embodies the experience of those long dead—a mummified experience. But among moral facts, that tangled and bewildering jungle, the inexperienced soul, if it is to escape peril, must be led by custom. To depart from that leading is adventure.

What proportion of mankind shuns adventure, what proportion courts it? The legislator wants to know, that he may increase the number of the cautious; the leader of men, that he may breed more adventurers.

This is the greatest and most significant division of mankind. It divides the givers from the takers, the doers from the done-by.

None, of course, is always giver or always doer; every life has its passive part. But there are natures in whom the active preponderates, and these are the adventurers, the creators, makers of many things, but above all of them, makers of experience.

They make it in the first instance for themselves; they drink the heady runnings of their own distillation from the still. Yet they also as well as others can taste the liquor, when it is mellowed and matured—perhaps modified by later blending.

All adventure is experience; that does not need to be argued. But adventure is enjoyed because it is experience. In all adventure, the whipping up of the blood, the stimulation of the nerves at the moment, is indeed a kind of physical pleasure, but the lasting charm is not there; it comes through a mark made on the mind, an impression on the sensitive complex of memory, that can be recalled and reproduced, enjoyed and studied at will.

The most obvious and primitive source of adventurous experience is danger. A child's first steps are surrounded by it, till experience brings confidence, and feet are planted firmly on the floor. That is the end of that adventure: new experience must be sought further afield.

Habit is a beaten path maintained by custom, and on it our lives run smoothly. Yet many are impelled to step outside it into the fields, even into primitive jungle, for the adventures that must bring experience. These know that they are less themselves when they are simply walking by some experience of the race which they have not verified for themselves by re-discovery, and to which they have added nothing.

This search for experience is a kind of privateering which the legislative mind will always condemn; yet without it the world would moulder. Failures in adventure are those who justify the proscription which they defied; who confirm that experience of the race which knows them for fools, or pursuers of nastiness from which they must be whipped off like puppies.

But the successful adventurer gains an experience which makes out of his adventure a lasting source of knowledge and strength for himself. In extreme cases he modifies, enriches, and enlarges the experience of the race: till by and by the legislator comes along and adores respectably what he wanted to burn.

These privateers very often have a tough time; the hardest adventures are not pursued on Mount Everest nor in big game shooting, nor in any sphere of physical danger.

Yet what is to be said about those moments when all habit breaks down; when the experience of the race finds itself up against a yawning gap in the permanent way—as has happened in our time? A friend of mine said that we should count ourselves fortunate to have been born when we were—to have been suckled when our mothers guessed so little the road that we must travel in, the doom we had to dree. My friend spoke in Ireland, which had its part of Europe's suffering, and then elaborated a neat purgatory of its own. Would we rather, even in Ireland, have avoided what had to come to us,—have lived in easier times?

The question is as futile as asking a man if he would rather be some one else. No doubt, this or that detail, external or internal, in our existence might be amended; yet none sinks so far in self-esteem as to desire total effacement of the only personality with which he is really acquainted. Indeed, we all want to be ourselves, because we cannot imagine being anyone else.

Nobody can speak for those upon whom war-time brought cruel separations. Yet there are many who would not refuse the name of privilege to a suffering which was recompensed in pride. Their experience may make them go softly all their days, but the world will seem to them nobler, not less endurable, by their own loss. No experience enriches more than admiration of those you love, and in thousands of lives death set on that admiration a seal which nothing can efface.

In our generation mankind, our race, faced as great dangers as willingly as ever since the world was. We can all say that; but those who loved, feel it: that is the fruit of their soul's adventure; that is their contribution to the race's gathered confidence in itself. Even those who have been frightened would hardly wish to have avoided this fear: it has, and they know it, enlarged their outlook on life. We all know more about life than we did, because we know more of death.

We have seen society strained and shaken, and in some countries, almost seen it broken; great political experiments, partly of advancing design, partly makeshift engineering to span a broken bridge, are in progress before our eyes: and we have seen how such a time intensifies the national character, as it does that of the individual. The Frenchman is more French, the German more German, the Englishman more English. In Ireland, where we always made a luxury of sardonic comment, the irony has entered into our bones, our life is penetrated with mockery: we chew a bitter cud. None envies us, none pities us: yet few Irishmen, I think, would honestly wish themselves into another age. The stimulus to curiosity is too keen, even among that vast majority, over whose lives the play was played.

Those who cry out against this surfeit of the unusual, the unexpected, the disturbing, and the dangerous, are no doubt mostly the votaries of habit, rich and poor alike; those contented in their misery no less than the more conspicuous persons who desired a stake-fence round their "stake in the country". Let us have peace: give us back a quiet life, is the cry of those who never wanted experience.

Yet everywhere in Europe are found true seekers after experience who have been disturbed from their own hunt. To read a new poet is an adventure, if he is new, and if he is a poet, and if you who read him can under-

26

stand. Before these brawls, your quiet intellectual went on his quest undisturbed: now the game he is after is scared away, his brooding thoughts scattered like snipe out of a bog when the first shot is fired. Before the war, some of these minds envied those who found it "bliss to be alive" in the days of the French Revolution: after it, they were deadly sick of adventures which to them had meant nothing.

Danger has no real teaching for you unless you are a specialist in the article: for the ordinary man, its prolongation, as he found in trenches, or in a bombarded town, is merely weariness. The physical, brutal adventure of dodging gunshot brings him nothing but crude chunks of undesired experience— more danger than he can digest. Facing danger means much if you are facing it with a purpose; if not, it merely exhausts the nerves and wastes that store of vitality which ought to be devoted to the life's true adventure, the inventor's, the thinker's, the artist's.

There is no such adventurer as the artist; every day is lost for him when he is not gaining experience; no one else is so intolerant of the fenced and trodden; if, as is often

27

true, the "trivial round will furnish all he needs to ask," it is because sun, moon and stars, wind and clouds, happy and unhappy faces, that to the commonalty would carry no experience, can bring an adventure to his spirit.

The quality of an adventure lies in the quality of the experience it leaves behind. For us all the war was an adventure profoundly modifying our experience and extending it; yet its very bigness made it an adventure of the race, rather than my adventure, or yours, or the next man's. A personal aspect developed, no doubt: one's first day in trenches was an adventure, having in it what the tourist in trenches also found there. Yet those who came for business were too busy studying their business to have leisure for appreciation: afterwards, trench warfare became a grim routine, deadening the faculty of apprehension without which there can be no experience gained. We learned; but most of what we learned was as elementary as what a child learns when it begins to walk alone: though for many generations our society had suppressed the need for these lessons.

Later, for instance in Ireland, came the experience of revolution and of civil war;

souls have not lacked material for adventure, and many of them have no doubt been enriched. Yet a looker-on gained little experience, except perhaps some added shrewdness in discerning which jockey to back. If adventures come to the adventurous, it is equally true that experience only grows when the soil suits it, when it comes to its own and its own receive it. Neither the war in which I fought, nor the civil war in which I did not fight, nor the revolution which I observed near by, held anything so properly an adventure for me as various adventures of peaceful travel. That experience was not crude lumps of something new and alien; it took root kindly and grew, it set up more continuous movement in my mind than many exciting scenes in politics or many an hour of shellfire. It was part of my real experience, the experience that I had sought.

I care not to have adventure thrust upon me, to have its form imposed: but I think nothing in life worth seeking or worth enjoying unless it brings experience: unless it adds to the colour and intricacy of the web that we weave on memory.

Having looked at the other ways, having experienced strife of party, strife of war, and known also, in and through them, the experience of comradeship, the tie of loyalty to a leader, my heart goes out to the quest that is pursued in peace and to the hope it offers. My allegiance is to the leaders in that adventure, my true comradeship with those who are of their band: who for the most part work with a lone hand, yet share with world what they acquire.

To have steeped the vision of summer twilight in the blue of eternity; to have put together some few words whose cadence will always reproduce a fine emotion, whose associated images will always evoke response in some sensibility, bringing remembrance of what we seem to have always known yet never perceived—that indeed is, after long adventure, to strain out the very essence of experience.

Yet often these doers and these makers do not know themselves for adventurers, and are scarcely aware that it is experience they bring home; the true labour, the true quest, passes far below the conscious mind. If brawls and wars hinder, as I believe they do, such adventures, and destroy unborn such outcome, then this is the most precious of all the commodities that they waste.

HATRED

CIVILISED Society has not yet abolished any of the vices, perhaps because it would be dull without them; but it does its best to eliminate passions, and in one case has virtually succeeded. Hatred as a passion, as something which takes and shakes a man, has no longer any real existence for the spheres of life in which urbanity is the rule.

In such regions, to avow your love is rather like undressing in public; but nobody is shy of proclaiming a hate, because what passes there for hate is not the crude stuff.

Love always retains some of the primitive all-conquering sway that Sophocles wrote about in another highly civilised society two thousand five hundred years ago, and even to-day no drawing-room is without apprehension that the creature may break loose.

It is not altogether a disagreeable apprehension: the discouragement of love is never whole-hearted; everybody, someone said, loves a lover, and at any rate every decent person does.

But hate with its acrid atmosphere carries discomfort into sensitive circles; its sudden explosion affects people like a bad smell, and so manners, much more powerful than morals, have brought it very tolerably under control.

Hate is not a necessity of nature; breeding earth has no use for it; and it runs counter to that instinct of association which is part of man's gregarious temperament. Thus it lacks the physical basis on which love is founded, whether between man and woman, or child and parent, and which spreads out till it colours even the clannish bond with something of kinship.

Yet one dare not deny hate's antiquity; it springs where love does, it dogs love like a shadow; jealousy is its first and fiercest form, growing as rank among kindred as among lovers. Cain was jealous. But as society is well aware, Cain lived and killed a long time ago; the world has grown wider, kinsmen who hate can easily avoid each other, and under social pressure they do so, instead of troubling company with manifestations of their rancour.

This concession to urbanity starves hate, deprives it of its natural food. As love fastens on whatever is individual and charming in bodily gesture, so you hate a man for his way of clearing his throat, or some other ugly or annoying trick. But in truth when his whole being is an offence to you, every action of his is a new grievance, and the nearer you live to him the more you loathe. From the town, where we have no fellowship with our neighbours, hatred, properly so called, has been almost banished; but it thrives profusely in Boeotia, which borders upon Arcady.

In a dull countryside you will not find man or woman readily owning up to a hatred, and still less will they parade the emotion. Hate, when it is the true passion, prefers to be disguised.

It was only in a society which did not fear this obsession that Dr. Johnson's phrase could be applauded. For, as everybody knew, when the doctor said he loved a good hater, that was part of his humour. No one was ever less likely to approve the person who would willingly inflict harm on another to gratify his own passion—and that is what hate means. Johnson might hate a Whig, or an atheist, or

an ungrammatical writer; but if you had produced before his eyes a suffering human, all
thoughts of Whig, atheist, or scribbler would
have vanished.

But I have known a prominent man who
became possessed of the power to ruin a
very insignificant political opponent. It was
pleaded that the victim had wife and children.
"Isn't the workhouse good enough for them?"
was the reply. That, now, was a good hater;
but would Johnson have loved him?

The truth is that Johnson was a typical
Englishman and the English are of all peoples
the least prone to hatred. Whether they
have succeeded by their good-nature, or are
good-natured because they have succeeded,
may be argued; but the fact is that for a very
long time they have felt no continuing need
of hate.

Whether hate be natural or no, it has
always been cultivated for man's extra-
natural purposes, in politics and theology.
Without these departments of activity, hat-
ing might be a lost art in civilised society,
gone like the power to track game or light
a fire by rubbing two sticks.

Christianity has always attempted to in-
culcate hate for the sin and love for the

34

sinner. But Christianity in practice keeps a strong Judaic tinge, and the Hebrew mind, for all its subtlety, never essayed this distinction, which should rank among counsels of perfection.

In politics, we are on clearer ground. Nobody there affects to behave like a Christian; indeed, we are all aware how necessary it is to be on guard against the seductions of decent feeling. "I never can hate a man properly after I've met him," said one of the most effective Irish politicians to me, giving his reason for avoiding intercourse with his opponents. He was only half joking; he knew his own dreadful liability to like and to be liked; he knew that the House of Commons tends to deaden by personal contact the intensity of party passions and to blunt the sharp outline of party beliefs. In that institution you inevitably become aware that the other side are not monsters of iniquity and that their opinion has something to be said for it.

Is this a merit or a defect? Merit, no doubt, if for the ordinary political uses of a well-established state; but defect, if you mean revolution. Ireland tended more and more to believe that Irish politicians who went to

Westminster lost something; and it was true. Except in rare and specially gifted individuals, hatred was sapped: and it would be foolish to deny that hatred is a driving force. No revolutionary movement has been able to dispense with it: the weaker the insurgent force, and the more strongly established the power which it seeks to overthrow, the greater will be the need of this stimulus.

Very little hatred seems to have entered into either of the two English revolutions, which were made by people exempt from the touch of hysteria which attends on desperate enterprises. Where there is no fear, there is not much hate. Napoleon frightened England into an hysterical passion for a while, and at the beginning of the last war the English, before they were certain of their resources, sought the aid of this dope. So also did Germany; though Germany's hysterical passion came perhaps less from fear than from the sudden jolt of an ugly surprise, like England's when matters went unexpectedly wrong in the South African War. But as the vast European struggle developed, the great Powers realised that their strength lay elsewhere, and the hymn of hate was little sung either in Germany, France or Britain.

It has been otherwise with those movements and those peoples that felt themselves overmatched. In Russia, who doubts that hatred was necessary to keep up the fight against autocracy? Ireland in a long wrestle was galvanised again and again to a sort of demoniac fury by preachers of hate, until finally she bit, kicked and tore herself loose.

But the drug habit is dangerous in morals as in medicine, and every revolutionary party is a forcing ground of private hates. It would be a fortunate conspiracy in which conspirators reserved their fiercest loathing for the power or person against which they conspired.

We know in Ireland, as probably they know in Poland, in Slovakia, in Russia, and a score of other countries where revolution has succeeded, what is the cost of a victorious hate. If the victory is a just one, if the revolution has been really due, the last and worst of injustices is that the victors come out demoralised by their victory. Where hatred has had free play, human nature is like the soil of an old battle line, upheaved, blasted and poisoned, the underworld brought on top, a surface which kindly growths abhor; and the rankest weeds take swift and spreading possession.

On the whole the House of Commons was the most civilising influence I have ever known, because hatred throve so ill there; and its most successful gladiator, who was also the most publicly hated man in his day, had the least capacity of all politicians for personal hate and the most power to undermine it. Mr. Lloyd George, I think, hated no one; and Mr. Balfour really fell from leadership, it seemed to me, because he could not hate Mr. Lloyd George; his intelligence was too accessible to seduction.

Stupid men are the best haters, because hatred is most solidly based upon misunderstanding. Party politics teach men to avoid considering how far they could agree with their opponents. The suppler, more adventurous intellect is more easily beguiled on to the forbidden ground, and once understanding begins, sympathy is apt to follow.

Yet hatred, whether public or private, has vision. The Irishman can see and foresee all the short-comings which beset the British temperament. But he will very seldom understand where an Englishman can be trusted to go right, and consequently will never get the best out of him.

All fruitful co-operation is based on the

expectation of good; expectation of evil is sterile, and that makes hate a barren passion. It is never an inspiration, never a creator of art, or of beauty in any shape; but it does desperately increase concentration. Benevolence is never focussed on one point like malevolence; it has too darting an activity; hatred is a fish that haunts slow, stagnant waters. It can hunt in packs too. I have heard of a sick salmon being devoured alive by eels; Parnell's last months were like that.

The French are too quick, too clever, really to be haters, in spite of some awful studies in Balzac, whose Cousine Bette is malignant, persistent, triumphant stupidity incarnate. But as a people the Germans will always out-hate them.

Few things are more characteristic of Germany, and less characteristic of England, than the dull old Hanoverian hatred of father for son, son for father, but especially of father for son. In the minds of the early Georges there were no gusts of intellectual curiosity or wandering adventure to divert the mind from what it chewed upon.

Agility is not a virtue, but it is a very useful habit; and it should be possible to invent a moral equivalent for physical drill to prevent the growth of morose brooding. Probably the religious orders have planned one, but Browning's Soliloquy of the Spanish Cloister is a dreadfully credible study of hate in idleness. That monk had never been hurried. And I have known a man, kindly, humorous, a thinker, and by his profession specially a Christian, yet become cankered, sour and unwholesome, because a hate took hold of him. He had suffered injustice, and yet worse men have often borne worse hardships better; but in his lethargic body and slow ruminating mind, the evil seed got too long a chance to establish itself, struck deep, and overspread all.

Yet his passion was ineffectual; it harmed no one but himself. Hatred may further a vicious man's purposes: it is of no use to a gentleman and can only spoil him. Mr. Galsworthy in one of his finest works, *The Man of Property*, shows the process by which a dull creature destroys a clever one. Bosinney has no more chance against Soames Forsyte than the fly against the spider. The man of property wins not only because all the material odds are on his side, but also because he has the more concentrated emotion.

The hate of those who want something

against those who have it is never so intense as that of those who have property against those who want it. The Tory hates the Radical better than the Radical hates the Tory, because hatred against those who, as you conceive, withhold from you abstract rights, is very much less vivid than the possessor's hate of those who would deprive him of things or privileges which have become part of him. Property on the defensive is like the bear with her whelps.

For Soames Forsyte the issue is complicated because the challenged and invaded property is a woman, his wife, and according to tradition, his hatred should be all the fiercer. Yet, and Galsworthy saw this, Soames cannot enjoy his triumph because he is too civilised, and particularly too civilised in ar English way. His hatred's victory is Pyrrhic, because he has been bred to the traditions of a gentleman. Decidedly the English are bad haters.

Shakespeare, who drew cruelty so often and with such varying skill, is in no way more English than in his lack of concern with this tremendous passion of hate. Capulets and Montagues are merely cat and dog to each other, and there is really not much

more subtlety in the portrayal of Shylock's
feeling against Antonio. In all the plays, Iago
is the only real hater; he can twist every
virtue of the Moor into a vice. He is hate,
as Othello is jealousy. Yet his master-passion
is not studied with the same subtlety as the
Moor's. We find Iago's hate full-grown; we
watch its workings; but we see the birth of
jealousy in Othello and its death also. I do
not recall anywhere in Shakespeare the growth
of a hatred sketched even so slightly as the
growth of Desdemona's love is sketched by
retrospect in Othello's speech to the judge.
Caliban again is hate at its most brutish;
there is no nobleness entangled with that
slime. Shakespeare was not at all of Dr.
Johnson's opinion. He was too near nature,
too little over-civilised, to speak pleasantly
of good haters. Yet perhaps Mercutio is one,
in Johnson's meaning: one could imagine the
huge dictionary-maker having a lusty detesta-
tion for "a puppy that fights by the book of
arithmetic". But in Mercutio there is none
of the black corroding venom, which may be
shameless and self-avowed, as in Iago or in
Caliban, yet which may also filter itself
unknown into the chalice.

Considering the range of Shakespeare's

scrutiny, it is notable that his imagination should have worked so little on this common and terrible corruption, and I think the true reason is that he was so English.

Probably the English have succeeded because they have been comparatively so free from this obsession. A man hag-ridden by hate is in a poor way to prosper. If you spend your life taking thought how to do some man, or some nation, an ill turn, your mind, vaulted in by its pre-occupation, will miss sight of those occasions when a friendly and profitable bargain may be struck, or even some good turn done that in all probability will beget another. These are the occasions which English seldomer let slip, and oftener catch hold of, than any other people in Europe.

THE VICE OF SOLITUDE

SOLITUDE, according to Aristotle, is only fit for a brute beast or a god. Yet man often inclines towards that for which he is not fit. There is no great harm in wanting to be a bird or a boa-constrictor, because you cannot bring it off; but a man can very easily, in the commonest figure of speech, make a beast of himself.

It bears out Aristotle's view that he can do this most effectively in solitude. Solitary drunkenness is bestial; social ebriety often has cordial qualities. The wittiest man I ever knew drank because wine stimulated his wit; it was not really drink he loved, but pleasure in giving pleasure.

Sexual vice at its worst seeks a brutish gratification which its partner is no more a companion than the gin-bottle. Where there is companionship, there is always the chance of comradeship, in which human life finds its human perfection. Solitary perfections there are, but we are aware of something inhuman about them; in the same way men will never

44

absolutely condemn actions which have something social in them. We have no indulgence for the solitary swindler or pickpocket; but stealing seems less dishonourable when there is honour among thieves. We have an instinctive sense that almost any companionship, even companionship in crime, is better than none for most mortals.

Instinct only forsakes us when we begin to work out moral prescriptions. Modern society believes that punishment is inflicted for the moral good of the offender; yet it punishes habitually by solitary confinement. We are going to make a new man of you, says society to the delinquent, and immediately subjects him to the regimen suited only to a god or beast. In short, we do not recognise the vicious quality which besets the inhuman state of solitude.

One should not deny the value of occasional tonic plunges into a cold well of silence; and there are exceptional natures which can constantly, and not merely on occasion, brace themselves in loneliness and by loneliness. Certain aspects of religion and certain superstitions fostered by literature, encourage us to regard the wilful solitary as somehow a seeker after the divine. Yet it is almost as

45

dangerous to try to make a god of yourself as a beast.

Many great religious leaders have laid down that if you seek for solitude you had best seek it in a community and under discipline. As to the pseudo-literary superstition that in order to be a great writer or great thinker, you should avoid social intercourse, was Shakespeare solitary? Burns solitary? or Keats? Shelley, who wrote so much about solitude, loved, though in his own queer way, "such society as was gentle, wise and good". Byron, for all his youthful misanthropic pose, was the best of company, and the only two among poets of the last century who really suffered from the vice of solitude were Edward Fitzgerald, for whom it became what opium was to Coleridge, and Tennyson, whose poetry and personality both showed traces of its evil effect.

In the sense that it is a danger and a vice, solitude is a state of mind, not a state of body; a deliberate shutting the self off from human companionship; not a discipline but a self-indulgence. That one may be more miserably alone in London than in the bleakest country is a truism; true also that self-indulgence in solitude is easiest in a great town. An absolute hermit of the wilds may be in communion with animals, wild or tame; if he has to feed himself, he knows the subtle but very real companionship of things that grow; and if food be brought him by human piety, then he would be a vicious solitary indeed if he were not conscious of the care by which he is surrounded and did not answer with grateful sympathy.

But a Londoner, from waking to sleeping, may be furnished with all the comforts his purse can pay for, and yet scarcely enter into one relation evoking human fellowship.

In the country, if you are served, it is impossible not to know and be known by those who serve you; if you want absolute loneliness there, you must work for it, and one need grudge no one the solitude that he has wrought out with his four bones: just as a man is not quite discreditably drunken on beer of his own brewing. But to issue forth of a morning, to get all services as automatically as you have turned on the hot water for your bath; to be carried from place to place at a word, or simply on the production of a coin (it matters nothing which, since the one with whom you deal is unregarding and unregarded as the machine which may replace

47

him); to have your food brought you by strangers; to pass your afternoon perhaps in a club where a snore is involuntary transgression, but conversation lacks that excuse; or, if there or elsewhere, before your day ends, speech becomes inevitable, to contrive that it shall be barren of companionship as the asphalt pavement is of grass—why, so to pass your time is to be a negative and unremarkable member of society. But every day of it converts a man increasingly to the vice of solitude.

As the crust about such a one hardens, how should laughter pierce it, or compassion, which is laughter's other face? The solitary will answer that laughing or crying never helped anybody; that he discharges faithfully the work of his office, is exact and trustworthy where money is concerned, fulfils his duty to society, and for the rest is self-sufficient. But he will not tell you, and he does not know, that in this imagined self-sufficiency lies the savour and the root principle of his vicious habit. The vice of solitude is not simple: it is a compound of sloth, self-deceit and pride.

For to be self-sufficient is good, yet there are things one cannot decently do without.

Washing, for instance, can for long periods be disused without detriment to the body, as we all found out in war; yet we blame the unwashed. The solitary, concurring in that verdict, would say that a man should not be disagreeable to his neighbours. But a repellent and unsociable presence is more disagreeable than most sights or even smells. One is not entitled to carry into normal society the mentality which might be appropriate for St. Simeon on top of his pillar. If you must be solitary, be solitary in good earnest; accept the material conditions of solitude; but do not expect to profit by the social machine and escape the first social obligation, which is not to be disagreeable.

You have no talent for being agreeable? Possibly, but no one is agreeable, just as no one plays billiards, without at some time taking pains. You may not succeed brilliantly, but you need not always cut the cloth. Many passable performers in human intercourse would have been as intolerable as yourself, had they been too arrogant for an effort, at least to avoid displeasing.

As for the pretence of an intellectual need to be isolated from disturbance, in ninety-nine cases out of a hundred it would not deceive a child; indeed, no one is quicker than a child to distinguish natural concentration of mind from sulky self-withdrawal. Very few work best in any real sense alone; and even for them the stimulus of contact with other minds in other spheres of thought is almost always useful. Yet it often happens that though an intelligence is naturally hospitable and sociable, the vice of solitude creeps in—a kind of foppishness, some touch of arrogance, helping sloth. The good of giving and taking in human intercourse is not denied, but there comes a disposition to say, "Will there be giving worth my taking?" or perhaps more often to think, "Will my giving be valued at what it is worth?"

For in the main this vice is one of advancing life. The young have morbid fits of shunning and despising society, but they are not all a pose; youth, with all its discoveries to make has many fields to make them in, the ferment in its own being keeps the brain hotly if obscurely at work. Later, in the growth of a healthy nature, desire to extend observation, desire to match itself against others, will always draw towards companionship. It is later that the temptation comes. So many curiosities have been gratified, so many disappointed in the course of life. We know, broadly speaking, what our own generation has to say to us. It is not always easy to be hospitable to the new generation of ideas: it is easy to expect from the new generation too much welcome, perhaps too deferential an acceptance for what we have to offer. Disinclination to renew touch with what seems already too well known, inclination to repel what seems raw, unlicked and unfamiliar, join to push us down the path which ends in a more or less complete intellectual isolation—and, what is worse, in a solitude of the emotions.

It will be said that man normally lives in a family, and the new generation is within his doors. Family life, it is true, involves a community of eating and drinking, of certain habits, of affections perhaps; but when a man has ceased to scour his wits out of doors, does he often keep them bright within? Uncompanionable abroad is very seldom good company at home. Cut yourself off from contact with the constantly renewing life of ideas, and your convictions ossify; so much everybody knows. But a worse thing comes when a man, after too long indulgence in a lazy and sulky solitude, finds himself in the presence of some great public emotion which he cannot feel. All that he is fit to feel is the disturbance and its discomfort.

When the bottom drops out of our carefully conserved social fabric, nothing but a strong force of sympathy or a long bracing of the mind by forecast can render the shock endurable to one whose habits have been long formed; and for the solitary, habit is the whole of life; he is alone with his habits. And so, in some vast emergency, he may, after all the talk of self-sufficiency, find himself no better than an uprooted parasite, whimpering that things might in decency at least have lasted his time.

Solitude is a kind of malingering. When the tough hour comes, you need to know at once, not who is for you and who against you —that is the leader's affair—but, clearly and decisively, whom you are for, whom you are against. Companionship will prompt you, comradeship which rests on so much more than habit will be your safe guide; but from solitude you are likely to emerge only that lame thing, a looker-on.

COURAGE

W E, as it chances, know more than our immediate forefathers about fear and fear's antidote, courage. Fear comes first. Where there is no fear there can be no courage. Plant-life swarming on a stalk feed tranquilly while their fellows are being eaten at their sides. There is no disturbance, no excitement, no resistance: the eaters have no courage, the eaten no fear. Higher in the scale, where the species is produced with less profusion, nature provides the arrangement by which living organisms are prompted to forecast disagreeable consequences, and especially death, which seems repugnant to the more developed possessors of life.

You get then the swift, tremulous ear-pricking creatures, the cautious burrowers, the simulators of a dead leaf; and you have the equally alert hunter, developing perhaps in the first instance courage to attack a formidable bulk.

But in its elementary forms courage has well-defined limitations. Rabbits fight valiantly among themselves, but the most valiant rabbit has no courage against a weasel's teeth, and, still more decisive, against the prestige of the weasel's tribe.

Nothing produces a dominant type of courage so readily as the consciousness of superior armament. The weasel, having spent life in killing creatures greatly larger and more powerful than himself, is puffed up with recklessness, and will turn in the mouth of his cranny to snarl at a man—an audacity through which many valiant weasels have become casualties.

Human beings find it hard to escape instinctive admiration for courage, whether in a weasel, or in the skilled revolver shot who has killed so many that he ceases to regard himself as subject to danger. His prestige like the weasel's, gives him incalculable advantage. Achilles, Du Guesclin, D'Artagnan, and the like could go into battle any day with a light heart, while it was very difficult to find courage to stand up against them.

In modern war no one has this personal ascendancy; the swordsman is obsolete, the marksman has little more chance than another of bringing his skin out whole. Consequently, the need for courage and the chance to be courageous are more evenly distributed.

We at least are rid of the illusion which haunted the later Victorians that physical courage in a race tended to become atrophied with disuse. Where they were guessing, we know. Almost every man between thirty and sixty has learnt to estimate his resistance to fear as accurately as the height he can jump; and women had the same knowledge very widely spread among them. In truth, courage never completely came to its own before our day as a moral quality; the courageous little fellow is no longer the bantam sparring up to a turkey cock, applauded and laughed at. Ajax was thought brave when he smote his way through the field of battle; he was thought mad when people found him defying the lightning. Millions of us, and often in our civilian life, were obliged to do as matter of routine what Ajax was thought mad for doing. And we could be courageous about it. You cannot fight the lightning or a Zeppelin bomb, but you can fight the real enemy, your own fear.

It is commonly said, and quite truly, that physical courage is by no means the most

interesting expression of this human quality;
but it is the simplest, and since we have been
given exceptional chances of observing it, we
should be fools indeed not to profit. Courage
does not really mean killing people or getting
yourself killed; either of those exploits can
be managed without it. It means controlling
your natural fear, which through imagination
magnifies every danger. It means that you do
not think about chances of danger when they
are negligible, as they may very well be,
though an inexperienced imagination would
think them appalling—say, in a London
street.

The normal man in war learnt to compute
his chances very reasonably. Going into a line
where five in a hundred men would probably
be hurt, he did not expect to be one of the
five. Experience helped him to combat fear:
yet there were cases where it stimulated
imagination disastrously. At a sentry post
where there was for that night no more risk
than at Charing Cross, I have seen sweat
running down a lad's face in the bitterest
cold; he had seen in the same environment
more than he could forget, yet it was no
more than his comrades had seen. He had
come as a volunteer, on a creditable motive,

to face dangers of which the whole world knew—and one could only be sorry for his failure, which carried its own punishment. The men with him hated him with a kind of animal loathing for the sick beast; they knew the contagion of fear—and the radiation of courage.

It is not courage alone that gives courage to others: it is courage with a happy heart. You would suddenly come on a knot of men where this atmosphere showed in the midst of physical misery; the next post to them might be dour fellows, unflinching, who pulled their full weight, but they pulled no more. There was also a mulish type, insensible to acute danger, which owed its courage to sheer lack of imagination: such men would always shirk the certainty of labour and discomfort if they could. Yet having been unafraid where they showed fear, they had a deep-seated conceit of their own valiancy: and probably justified themselves for malingering by this perverse pride—as after all Ajax did, if not Achilles. We ask more of our heroes than the ancients did, and we get it.

Physical courage in actual modern war has at least become more of a purely moral quality, and less of an ascendancy in slaughter.

Those were followed and loved who went gaily into danger with thought for all but themselves. The gayest and coolest that I knew moved carelessly under a premonition of his own fate: he died, as he had expected, by gas poisoning. I do not think he ever received any decoration, but it is of him and his like, that his little machine-gunners and their like think when they speak of physical courage.

Probably all the millions of us who shared those experiences attach too high a value to this quality. Yet since the price was heavy, do not let us decry what we have gotten. And civilians who went through a serious air raid tranquilly would, more easily have stood up against trench bombardment, where discipline, the will of others, tradition and suchlike buttresses, kept a man erect; moreover, the armed soldier had at least the illusion of being able to strike back.

If after all this has passed, we—soldiers or civilians—can find ourselves not deficient by the decent normal standard, which we have all learnt to apply—well, it is something to know that we have our decent share of what the world has always valued.

Modern war is horrible, but it has this redeeming feature, its duties lie nearer to citizenship than soldiering ever did in the past. There was no sharp dividing line where civil and military parted. Each nation made was as a nation: and perhaps, as a consequence, discipline carried further than ever before that conception of courage in which a man has to abandon all separate thought for himself.

We may be certain that in the Stone Age nobody who could run away faced annihilation by irresistible force: in the heroic literatures, to do so was regarded as the extreme of heroism; yet in our modern times countless thousands advanced to destruction, having learnt to regard survival and victory as a matter for the side, not for the player.

It is said that war has brutalised us, has deteriorated instead of ennobling; and in particular that it has afflicted society with a multitude of dangerous desperadoes. Certainly the discontented men are more discontented and more dangerous: I am not sure that they are morally the worse. War taught hundreds of thousands to value themselves on the possession of proved physical courage, and to regard themselves as better men than those whose courage is not so proven. But it taught them also that what they faced they faced as a civic duty.

Those who blame the discontented most loudly were loudest in creating illusion: for it is an illusion that courage can be paid for. As well expect to be rewarded for health, of which indeed courage is a form.

In some future age, when courage is made perfect, men will realise that there is no pay coming and none needed for this excellence. It may help you indirectly to promotion. But the true reward of physical courage is the prestige which it gives with others, and the confidence which it begets in a man, who knows that in one matter anyhow he can count on himself.

To master imagination of danger in its crudest and roughest forms is at least a good beginning to abolish all fear. And if fear were gone, most paths of life would be easy walking.

II

Physical courage is a revolt against Nature's instinct of self-preservation: yet it is also natural; animals must fight to live; all need it. Moral courage is a revolt too, but not against Nature: it is a revolt against the second nature of habit.

To discard your coat in London on a hot June day would be natural, but would require moral courage beyond what most of us possess.

When society praises moral courage, it is stimulating the enemies of society; for moral courage is very often, in a sense, immoral. Morality sums up the moral judgments of society, that is, of people at a certain date and place; so to disregard what others think is to disregard morality. However, society, like the individual, must take risks, for without moral courage morality can neither be maintained nor improved.

Yet society is well aware of its risks in this matter. To reward physical courage may be fostering the bully; to approve moral courage may be nourishing the rebel, and from society's point of view the rebel is much the more formidable danger. It has no fear that the instinct of self-preservation will disappear, and consequently it rewards physical courage, sometimes lavishly; the moral quality is always exempt from remuneration.

One may indeed argue, that moral courage imposes its own standards, by which reward would be almost an insult. Yet the proportion of truth is not big enough to save this reasoning from a colour of cant. Let anyone compare his own feelings, or hers, towards the Victoria Cross man and towards the perfectly conscientous conscientous-objector.

Assume the best in each case. Assume that the soldier has expected to be killed in his effort to save life; assume, on the other hand, that the objector had a brave man's sensibility to reproach. Is it really a harder thing to risk life than to face the ignominy of refusing to risk it when millions are taking that hazard?

All the logic in us may go out to the rebel against war, but can it carry our feelings with it? If it could, the rebel would have won, and society would be his following.

In primitive society, freedom can hardly be said to exist: all is custom that is not brute force. What freedom there is in the world, man has won for himself.

Custom has established what moral courage won; but the same courage has been needed again to extend conquests, even against the police force. Every ordinary citizen is the custodian of custom, and the more ordinary he is, the better policeman. The policeman

may, and does, use moral suasion, especially
with those under excitement, political, religious or alcoholic; but he must not himself
be open to conviction by even the most
engaging arguments, or society would collapse.

Policemen are not perfect, the most ordinary citizen will at times experience conver-
sion, and consequently society does at times
collapse: it is in truth continually crumbling
under the attacks of moral courage, and continually being propped up by the same
quality.

For moral courage has both an offensive
and a defensive aspect. It is the instinct
which teaches men to uphold an honoured
principle in a society grown lax about that
article; yet it will also challenge a rule of
action in a society that upholds it. In either
case society will be against the morally
courageous man; it would be silly to speak
of courage when there is no danger.

Yet it is part of courage to estimate danger
justly, and a good share of mankind's moral
conquests have been won by recognising
phantoms for what they were. Rome, the
great builder, was before all a builder of
usage; but it was one of the greatest Romans

who realised what mankind owed to the
rebellious moral courage of the Greeks. In
all literature nothing is finer than the passage
where Lucretius describes the terror of those
phantoms against which Greek humanity first
lifted up a visage of defiance.

The ally, or the instrument, of conquest
was reason; the enemy was imagination: and
Lucretius saw that courage of the intellect
pitted individual reason against the amplified,
elaborated and consecrated imagination of the
whole race. To go out against gods or devils
was an incomparably bigger deed than to fight
your fellow-human; and it was none the
smaller because you came back victorious,
having proved that neither god nor devil stood
against you to fight.

Yet this is only one aspect of the praise
due to pioneers. Early in all histories it
needed physical courage to be a moral rebel,
for the man who disregarded custom and what
Lucretius called religion was knocked on the
head by his fellow-citizens. Perhaps the most
remarkable achievement of moral courage is
that it has established a right to be fought
with its own weapons. In the extreme case
of conscientious objectors, British conscience
would not allow them to be killed; it did not

really like them to be physically maltreated. But it used against them with enthusiasm all the weapons which public opinion feels entitled to wield against the rebel, and they are terrible enough.

Moral courage when it stands on the defensive to assert clean traditions in the midst of slovenliness, trickery, peculation and sexual cynicism, finds ridicule loud against the precisian or the puritan. Some artist, some thinker, is always ready to assail his own kind.

Yet they are his own kin; for every artist is, at least, at first, a rebel; he wants to live his own life, play his own play, be himself; and society always begins by thinking him an imbecile or a loafer, and applauds his established fellow-craftsman, who makes songs against the new singer. Aristophanes has the laugh, and the crowd with him, against Socrates or Euripides ever and always.

Still the rebel can use ridicule: witness Voltaire and numberless others; and perhaps the attacker, rapier against cutlass, has held the deadlier steel.

But ridicule at its hardest is no more than moral courage can easily confront: nobody is seriously afraid of the policeman's baton, but of the gaol he stands for. In the moral world, gaol's equivalent is the boycott, society's legitimate weapon. If the rebel starve, well, whose fault? Moral courage has to include readiness to face every material privation; and here it borders very closely on the physical, and is allied to that form of courage which must dare to take risks with the lives of others.

One who to serve a cause brings hunger on his dependents may rank for courage with the statesman who justly decides that his country shall make war. Perhaps he should rank higher, if his cause be worthy; for the rebel has custom's whole weight against him, while tradition is generally a main motive for beginning or continuing a war.

Finally, moral courage must face the purely moral terror which lies in the censure pronounced by others. Here the brave man easily enough disregards the opinion of those whose opinion he does not value? But it is a hard thing to be sent to Coventry by your pleasant friends; a harder, if those who love you, and whom you love, condemn, or even despise you. There may be, there often is, only one judgment that matters, and when that goes against you, courage is tried indeed.

It is bad enough when mutual material interests are involved and you seem to be inflicting ruin for a reason not admitted as sufficient; harder, perhaps, for some, where religion is involved and all the attendant pieties; but hardest of all assuredly when there is disagreement concerning honour. To crown all, the opinion that counts with you so much may be buttressed up by the opinion of all your world.

Yet in truth that addition makes little matter: the essential conflict is the single clash that you would give your life to avoid.

In such a duel, what is victory? To make your opinion prevail? Rather, I think, to win freedom for your opinion; and your right to act on it. The best proof that you have conquered freedom is that you do not seek to enforce your conception of it where you would most desire that it should be shared.

The mother of a soldier who resigns his commission at war's outbreak may not admit the reasoning on which he acts, yet, through her knowledge of him, she may recognise his courage and love him more, not less. If so, both will have gained a victory; yet not unless she admits that he may possibly be right.

When a moral standard is challenged by a moral courage that defies all the consequences, there can be no immediate certainty of judgment: moral standards are constantly being changed under the challenges of moral courage. There is only one test. Unless the rebel is willing that his action should establish a rule for others, the Apache is morally as brave as he.

Habitual defiance of usage in petty affairs is a kind of moral swashbuckling; that is the way to be a crank. Those who never disagree lightly with their fellow workers, yet will speak their mind and act on it in vital matters, seldom need to display their courage because their firmness is known.

In its highest forms courage does not dwell on physical ordeals but assumes the will to face death as almost a necessary consequence of serious belief. When action begins, risks have all been faced in the mind beforehand; the cost has been counted; imagination is busy only with the means to its end. Courage has conquered its enemy, imagination, in imagination's own territory.

EDUCATION

EDUCATION offers probably the earliest applications of the factory system; the single schoolmaster was the germ or cell out of which the perfect modern education establishment developed. Since male evolution is always in advance of female, the boys' school preceded the girls' school, as the tailor preceded the dressmaker.

Males were produced according to a pattern, which, though accepted in the home, was not designed there, at a period while females were still being shaped in primitive fashions to respond to the actual needs of life. Females were trained, with a primitive humility, for what they had to do, by watching it done and by doing it, while the school was setting out to teach their brothers not to do, but to Be.

Where life remains primitive, education is the training of the son by the father to follow the father's business, and of the daughter by the mother to follow the mother's. This education is carried out much more by imitation of example (under correction) than by precept. But at an early period pride operated, and the vainer sex must be held responsible for the ambition which, not content with doing, aspired to Be.

Doing was a humble business, readily acquired at home; but learning was in the first instance, as in other days, a branch of Being. The learned might not be able to do much, but they were more powerful, more admirable, more respectable.

There was, indeed, some pretext of a definite purpose. Scholars were quite early taken into professional schools and trained for the priesthood or the law: but that again was training to *be* priests or lawyers, not to *do* anything of concrete and unquestionable usefulness. The concrete utilities were looked after at home.

Nobody knew this better than the schoolmaster; and the one thing really practical about his trade was the manipulation of those standards by which his output would be judged.

Society got one man to teach its boys, just as it got another to make tools or clothes. But the proof of boots is in the wearing, of a spade in the digging: what test could be applied to the schoolmaster's work?

If after his years of schooling a boy was of no more practical use than before, plainly the teaching trade was endangered. I have no doubt that some early schoolmaster first had the defensive idea of saying, "But see what a fine fellow I have made him." If the parent could not see, the schoolmaster, taking a high tone, publicly set that down to his ignorance.

Professional educators, with Plato at their head, implanted in the European mind a belief that education is, in the mediæval sense, a mystery, a craft with its own secrets, amenable only to judgment by its initiated. If the factory system was applied in education much earlier than in other trades—if the tailor still worked single-handed in his shop, when already at Athens or Rome you had in the school a head operator directing ill-paid assistants—the reason is, I think, that educators early felt the need of creating a caste to protect their mystery.

Plato was a long way from the perfection to which our days have attained, but his grasp on the essential parts of advertisement was firm and thorough. He avoided undertaking that which the pedagogue is quite unable to perform. If the object of education is admitted to be *doing* something, progress can only be made through imitation and observation, which are directed mainly by the sub-conscious mind; and the sub-conscious insists upon learning nothing but what it wants to learn.

But Plato, being proud, was determined that boys should learn what he thought good for them. No pedagogue ever repudiated more completely anything that could be called low, mechanical or utilitarian; and, knowing well that the ruck of human beings were low and utilitarian and concerned about *Doing*, not *Being*, he insisted that education should be removed from the demoralising influences of home. The human raw material must go to an educational factory and there be fashioned to a standard pattern of nobility.

Yet being wise, and a Greek, he shaped this pattern conformably to certain instincts of the sub-conscious, and especially to the instinct for beauty and rhythm.

Like every other theorist, Plato had something concrete to stimulate his imagination. He had Sparta.

There is no proof that success followed

application of the Spartan system to his own much more complicated purposes of culture; but the Spartan methods, as interpreted, or rearranged, by Plato's fantasy, have been the guiding inspiration of European education on the factory system, and especially in these islands.

To eliminate home influence was to be Spartan: but the English public schools greatly bettered their instruction. The English public schoolboy was much more cut off from his home than can ever have happened to the young Spartan, who lived in the same township with his parents.

Of course, whether in Sparta or in England, something came of it. When a mass of young humans are brought together and kept together, employed upon academic pursuits (we owe that word "academic", with so much else, to Plato), and are thereby segregated for a considerable period from the business of production, that is, from Doing, and consequently concentrated upon Being, education goes on. But even in these unnatural conditions, education works by nature's way; training comes through imitation. Education in the home is the education of the young copying their elders. Education in an educa-

73

tional factory is the education of the young
copying the young.

Public opinion among the young is modified
by the less important public opinion of their
parents; but this has less and less effect in
proportion as the separation from home is
longer and completer, till, in the best type
of English public school it may be regarded
as negligible.

When this public opinion (so modified, or
so unmodified) is in favour of learning to
pass examinations, which is what an educational factory officially strives to teach, the
young will as a rule learn to pass them. It
happens so in France, where most pupils are
day boys, and the home influence, for what
it is worth, is used in that direction. In
England, where public opinion, alike among
the young and their elders, regards the
acquisition of this learning as unimportant,
the young as a rule do not progress very far
in it.

But in either case, while the factory is
teaching boys to *do* nothing except to pass
examinations, education in Being goes on
apace, for good and for bad. "Gentleness and
kindness, these are the perfect duties, these
come before all morality", said Stevenson;

EDUCATION

I am not sure that gentleness and kindness are specially well learnt in an educational factory.

If Being is the object of education, I incline to think that boys will achieve it better by living at home than by transplantation into a little artificial world where everything is fictitious and precocious: where they must very often fight merely to be let alone, or must give up freedom to avoid fighting.

For in the educational factory we always come back to Sparta, and glorification of the will to fight. The English-speaking culture used to maintain that avoidance of this public school tradition made an effeminate race, and we were pleased to look down on the French. Now, perhaps, we have the grace to recognise that England would scarcely have stood better than France the ordeal of having enemy trenches fifty miles from the capital during a period of four years.

But whether the application be complete, as in England, or incomplete, as in France, methods of the factory are applied to educating almost the whole of what is called distinctively the educated class in Europe.

The father's share in education tends to disappear: a man's knowledge of his own

business counts for less and less in the training of his own son; he sends his firstborn to
Rugby or Cambridge that he may learn to
be something different from what he would
have become, had the plastic period of his
youth been spent in close day to day observation of that which it will be his business
to *do*.

The soldier's vocation has been largely
hereditary in Great Britain, and the doctor's
and the lawyer's; in all these cases the
father's part in education has been greatly
and usefully formative.

Yet in a general way, a father now-a-days
is actually shy of trying to teach his son; the
mother perhaps a little less, but still increasingly diffident towards her daughter. What
was the most natural thing in life comes to
be regarded as an interference, almost as an
impertinence.

A woman does still regard it as possible to
make her own clothes, or to educate her
daughter. But an educated man regards
everything to do with education as being as
remote from him as the tailor's function.

There is, however, one form of *doing* which
the English public school teaches most effici-
ently—but a form of Doing closely related

76

to Being. It teaches how to keep school, to be a schoolmaster, of the English type. What is the British administrator but the British public schoolmaster writ large? excellent at distributing justice, and at maintaining order in a good-humoured way among subjects who are (from his point of view) imperfectly grown up. These he will gradually and firmly shepherd towards acceptance of his own ideals: he will make school prefects of the selected: but he will never admit or acknowledge their right to be, or desire to be, what he himself is not. To be perfectly grown up, in his eyes, you must be British; and that is perhaps the limitation to his excellence and to the value of the education which he gives.

Admitting that the real training of the British schoolmaster or administrator begins at school, for the rest of us the factory postpones education in Doing to a period immensely later than that which nature indicates.

The peasant cannot remember when he began to acquire the skill for his life's work: almost as soon as he could walk, he was absorbing through the pores what generations had accumulated. But we of the educated

classes push our apprenticeship in Being
(supplemented, if we are lucky, by learning
how to learn) till we are well past the age
at which men officially become soldiers: and
in four cases out of five, only then do we
begin to learn our special job.

We console ourselves by thinking that at
least we have been trained to *be*. Alas, when
the professional instructors in the art of Being
drop their task, when the stage of doing
things that have only a symbolic importance
is over, nature takes us seriously in hand. In
the civilised world, far more than in the
primitive, real education means the education
of adult man by adult woman, of adult woman
by adult man. By no other influence is the
quality of our lives so profoundly affected
and modified. And do not suppose that this
is education in Being, though we, with illu-
sions of the academy clinging about us, talk
of "being" in love. Nature has no concern
with Being: she intends action, she means
things to happen. And they do.

On the other hand, all life is education to
those capable of it, and the more civilised we
are, the longer we remain supple to learn.
Primitive man is scarcely educable after early
manhood: custom grips him: you cannot get

a new ply into the substance of the peasant after he has taken the mould. The characteristic of the most distinctive moderns is their prolonged teachability. Mr. Lloyd George was fifty in 1914, and probably knew as little of war or foreign affairs as any minister that ever sat in a British Cabinet. Like him or no, there is no disputing but Mr. Lloyd George came of what is so rare in Great Britain, peasant stock. It makes the strength of France. An amazing number of France's foremost men come from an ancestry trained in Doing: either directly from the land, or from a line of craftsmen, artisans who were their own masters. Sons of such people, when they leave the land or the workman's bench and go to an educational factory, have in their blood and bones the instinct for Doing: they go to learn how to learn, they assimilate knowledge with a fruitful intention, and their careers are the best justification that the educational factory can show for its existence.

Yet when we count the successes, can we reckon the waste? I believe we should have a better world if theorists in education followed nature's hint and developed, instead of avoiding, the natural method. General culture can quite well be made to grow out of special training instead of aiming to add apprenticeship as a separate story to a common base with many variations at top.

This change would in many cases restore to the parent his natural place in education. Unless indeed the factory has by now unfitted the parent for his natural function.

IN DEFENCE OF LUXURY

IN a bleak June, the bleaker after a torrid May, I permitted myself the luxury of a fire, and felt it the more a luxury because I felt it permissible.

It was a wood fire, and a wood fire has gaiety and brightness denied to coal; in winter it may come a little short in warmth, but in summer gives precisely what the human creature wants: it changes the atmosphere rather than the temperature. Any fire lover will appreciate the delicacy of this difference. Yet there are many to whom a fire is simply a fire, just as to others wine is simply wine, whether it be Moselle or Burgundy. These miss something exquisite, and are objects for compassion like those who cannot take pleasure in beauty.

Is beauty also a luxury? There are two pictures in the room where I write: things seen by Grace Henry through a temperament which transforms them into something rich and strange, so strange that it repels many. Yet to me they are among the greatest of my luxuries, chiefly because I have—in all humility—learned to enjoy them. Luxury is a privilege which you may earn by becoming capable of it; and you are not capable unless you are aware that it is a luxury.

This awareness may be helped and heightened from without. My generation was brought up to think fires in summer a wanton extravagance; and there is a luxury in knowing that what you enjoy is counted extravagant, which becomes honest and creditable if you feel that you have earned your privilege. I had earned my fire; it was like early peas from our garden, which we ate with greater enjoyment because, if we bought them, we should be living beyond our means. The tree that made the fire grew in our narrow bounds, and was condemned for reasons of utility, against which no sufficient plea of beauty could be urged; I cut it and stacked it; the fire to which I treated myself was my own work, product of my leisure; it even helped my business, for it is hard to write if one is chilly of a morning. Of course, one can do without it: if the fire were a necessity, it would not be a luxury. But it was a good part of the luxury to give myself dispensation for the indulgence.

Modern ethics, which challenge every proprietary satisfaction, will put an end to such gratifications. None of us will decide to cut a tree, for none of us will own one; none will permit himself a fire because the State will regulate all that, probably with a Victorian thumb on the almanac: in short, communistic ethics will abolish luxury; there will be no exceptions, no privileges, nothing but rules. Is that good or bad?

It would be more reasonable to ask, is it possible? Can you abolish luxury? Can you rigorously, logically, and effectively deny to all the satisfaction of the superfluous? *De grâce, laissez-moi le superflu.* Like all the really witty, that French aristocrat was a philosopher; his wit challenged authority to define what is meant by necessaries—or, for that matter, by life.

Is a luxury what you cannot afford? or simply what you enjoy but can do without? I could not afford my Grace Henrys, no civil tribunal would acquit me of extravagance; but the same judges would give my rich neighbour a certificate of character if he had bought them instead of me—all the more if he did not want them. They would call that "encouraging the arts". Or they might praise him for a wise investment. Odious reasons.

If the rich man gives his money to make an artist's work publicly accessible, he does good. But to buy, and lock up in his house that which he has no use nor care for, is to kill beauty, under plea of serving art. An artist is not a postulant for charity; his purpose is to earn by ministering to our refined enjoyments; and if you acquire from him that luxury which you are not fitted to taste, you sterilise his work. Or when your patron is the prudent man who makes a good investment, he buys cheap through the artist's necessity what he perceives that many will desire. This is legal, this is defensible, but it is not nice. The less good the investment, the fewer the possible competitors, the better was my right to acquire what I wanted, a beauty that to me was significant; and if I were the only person in the world who cared to have these things, my justification would be perfect; for the ideal luxury is that which deprives no one else.

If, as is more than possible, these luxuries of mine come to be eagerly sought after, I should resent praise of my prudence, and would rather boast of an imprudence which at least proved a feeling for their beauty. To have made a sacrifice, or taken a risk, for that which you want but can do without, enhances the luxury almost as if you had grown it in your garden.

On this count, then, neither civil tribunal nor any other form of authority can touch my conscience—though they would like to. But about my wood fire, any civil tribunal would puff up my self-righteous glow; yet I feel less secure. If the recording angel came and said: "You cut your tree to clear your ground; were there no poor neighbours, resentful of charity, who would gladly have carried away its branches—to oblige you? Did you not grab their necessity to provide your luxury?" It would be no use telling that angel that I needed the branches for pea-stakes.

But to pamper conscience is a luxury entirely beyond my means. Where are you going to stop? Nowhere short of communism, which is primitive Christianity, administered by a State-paid and uniformed police: and so, not primitive Christianity.

Is it unchristian to be thankful for luxuries? I mean unprimitive Christian, since every endowed and respectable church teaches that we should be thankful for whatever we have legally got, and should pray to be able to keep it legally. For what else should we be thankful than for luxuries? Is it really expected that we should say grace for necessaries? As well ask a baby to say grace for being born. The old-fashioned, but not at all primitive Christian, education taught children to say, "Thank God for my good dinner." Appreciation was implied; it was gratitude for a luxury. The infant mind, being very logical, understood that thanks were not rendered simply for a dinner; even when the dinner had not been enjoyable, it understood that one must be polite.

Mature minds understand that every good dinner is a luxury, if there is intelligent appreciation. It may be a refined and justifiable luxury to dine once in a way with extravagance; but I would rather dwell on the example of an old Frenchman who always insisted that there should be coarse salt on his table. *C'est mon luxe*, he used to say; the finely-powdered article had not the savour which his cultivated sense demanded; the rough cheap thing was a luxury, because he got from it a gratification that was not part of life's inevitable routine.

In truth, expense has little to say in the matter. A luxury is what a man feels to be a luxury. To me claret is far more of a luxury than champagne and quite as much a luxury when claret is cheap. A scientific lady proved (to her own satisfaction and mine) that wine was the best of brain-foods. Admirable woman. There is no better benefactor than one who can present as a condition of efficiency the indulgence for which you might be blamed. Many doctors, I fancy, have earned gratitude and reputation by such advice. Contrast this with the political philosophy which lays down that necessaries shall be exempt from taxation, and claps a duty of ten times its value on tobacco. There must be in England, there are certainly in Ireland, many thousands, who would like meat and never buy meat, yet buy tobacco as a matter of course: craving it perhaps the more because they know it is not indispensable—not a simple stoking of the machine.

I would not concede to the politicians their claim to decide what is essential and what superfluous to civilised humanity. As for taxing luxuries, they cannot. One of the saints that I have known was an elderly Irishman, who had lost his leg from the hip

down in the service of a petty Irish railway
company—mean as well as petty, for they
gave him such compensation as left him
barely able to pay for his keep in the house
of other pensioners. All was scarce, yet he
never stinted tobacco and he had his luxury:
but it was not the taxable weed. Near his
chair by the hearth was always a pile of dry
twigs: he would never light his pipe with a
match; it "left a taste on the smoke"; and
as for paper spills, somehow he "did not
care about them". But the light crackling
flame of the twigs, and a faint suggestion of
the wood every time that he reddened his
bowl, gave the little extra touch of enjoyment
that made his necessary into a luxury and
helped the cripple to keep a flow of merry
wisdom.

It has often become a luxury to do without
that which your predecessors thought indispensable; for instance, not to wear a top hat
—till this privilege became so common that
no one could be aware of it. This hat was
a symbol rather than an article of dress. You
acquired it, or you dispensed with it, at a
cost: you bought with it the luxury of feeling
respectable; in dispensing with it, you
acquired the luxury of unwonted comfort at

a sacrifice of respectability. Few indulged in the latter luxury unless they had a great balance of respectability at their bank.

A luxury may easily pass into a bondage; dressing for dinner is an example. So, as many discovered in the war, is the daily morning tub. The war taught many what we could abandon without loss, and, on the other hand, whetted some blunt perceptions; we know now the true worth of simple luxuries like sugar. It has not indeed killed the stupid desire for possession of what others cannot have (nothing will ever persuade me that diamonds are a luxury to the refined); but it opened many eyes to the genuine luxury of splendour, of elegance, of exquisite cleanness. Many a man learnt in hospital, as never before, how great a luxury is the sight of pretty clothes, enhanced by the pleasure which they give to their wearer. Yet the luxuries one would soonest defend are those which, as the phrase goes, cost nothing.

Freedom is the universal possession which we would all rather die than sacrifice; and it is very hard to take it from you. You may part with your garments of ceremony, your comforts, your pictures, your books, even

with much liberty of action, and still retain
the luxury of free speech. Yet most find that
too dear for their possessing: they surrender
it to keep their motor car, their diamonds.
Even when free expression is gone, there lies
in the last reserve one most intimate indulgence—the practice of shaping your own
thoughts, instead of getting them ready-made
from the Press, the pulpit, or some other
factory. It is dangerous; it may lead to
putting thought into word, or even into act;
but it is a luxury by my definition. You enjoy
it; and the mass of mankind does very well
without it.

PIETY

IT is surprising how variously some words
wear, especially those which express moral
appreciations. "Good", of course, and
"bad" are simple as a child's first judgments;
and though personal accent, or literary skill
can make these primeval adjectives sum up
the whole of praise or condemnation, yet the
word then is gesture rather than speech.

But there are others, hardly less old, which
keep the first freshness of creation. "Kind",
"merry", "gentle", it needs no art for them
to be eloquent; they carry a caress from all
the generations, for about these qualities
humanity was never in two minds.

"Honest", "frank", "true", "loyal", these also
keep their ring imperishably; no skill is
needed to draw it out.

On the other hand there is a whole group
of words, which from the first deliberately
conferred the stamp of an inner circle; and
naturally these lack the large human weight
and force. Yet among them there are many

degrees of survival. "Charming" holds its own, for charm never goes out of fashion; while "elegant" is nearly obsolete, though the noun is less demoded than the adjective.

"Genteel" is the classic example of a poor word that comes down in the world till it can be produced only for uses of derision. Yet, though "gentility" has gone with it into limbo, we are more attached than ever to "gentleman".

That is, I think, because "gentleman" used to mean a man born into a certain rank, and only by implication, one who followed instincts and principles of honour suited to his rank. To-day the word has less to do with birth than with behaviour. Democracy accepts it.

The accompanying "gentlemanly" and "gentlemanlike" date only from the time of the "first gentleman in Europe". Macaulay disliked them as novelties and Lady Holland said she "could never break Sheridan of 'gentlemanly'." In fact, the adjective never quite made good, and now is nearly as obsolete as Regency pantaloons.

"Polite" survived, but a hundred years ago it used to convey an ideal; now it means what is the least expected of you in decent society. "Fashionable" has not lost or altered its meaning; it has merely gone out of fashion.

But there are words from a very different group, having noble associations, words of dignity and power, which yet seem somehow tarnished by an advancing shadow of disrespect.

"Virtue" is a great name. Yet most of us would rather be commended for our kindness or our goodness than for our virtue: while "virtuous" is actually apt to disparage. It has a smugness, and it is often used with a shade of irony, as when one speaks of "virtuous indignation". But what spoils it chiefly is too close association with the idea of sex. When English delicacy, avoiding the words "chaste" and "chastity", gave to "virtue" or "virtuous" almost a medical significance, they injured more than the language.

But we are in danger of losing altogether another adjective and noun, closely related to "virtue" in significance, yet having a special shade of meaning which no other terms can convey. "Pious" is shockingly defaced, and "piety" is only preserved by a very specialised usage.

Most of us can only employ these words

93

for praise by a sort of metaphor, describing the religious observance of what is not a religion:

> "Be ours the quest of a plain theme,
>   The piety of speech."

No one denies that Stevenson had this "piety of speech"; but would you call him a pious writer? All librarians would like to be praised for pious care of the treasures in their custody; but not all would wish to be described as pious men. In truth, it has come to this that very few of us, even hardy church-goers, would like to be so described. And this shyness of the word does not date from yesterday. When Walter Scott was on his deathbed, he said to Lockhart: "My dear, be a good man, be virtuous, be religious, be a good man. Nothing else will give you any comfort when you come to lie here." It is inconceivable that Scott speaking thus to Lockhart could have used "pious" instead of either of the words he chose to make clear what he meant by "good". But Dr. Johnson might have.

Both "pious" and "piety" are Protestant words. After the Reformation, they were gradually appropriated by the genius of the

94

language to the peculiar quality which under the influence of Protestantism the religious temper developed in England. "Pious" does not express the temper of the English Reformation, which had the fierceness of a revolution. You will not find it in the Authorised Version of the English Bible; it was no part of the vocabulary of the divines who naturalised the Hebrew scriptures so that for generations they coloured all English life and thought. Yet "pious" was current in the language of their day, for Shakespeare uses it freely.

It had come in from another source: it derived from the book which probably ranked next in influence to the Bible. Everybody who learnt anything beyond reading, writing and arithmetic, learnt Latin, and everybody who learnt Latin read about the pious Æneas. But very few of them learnt enough Latin to realise what *pius* meant to Virgil. English literature makes it plain that Æneas was considered to be pious because he carried his father on his back out of burning Troy— which was no more than any clansman in any country would have done for the chief of his clan. Virgil, of course, meant a great deal more, and chiefly, I think, wanted to dis-

95

tinguish Æneas, his ideal patriot, from Homer's heroes, but especially from Ulysses. All through the Odyssey Ulysses is asking the gods to help him accomplish his own will; all through the Æneid, Æneas is labouring to forward the will of God. An English word which expresses this larger sense of *pius* comes a thousand times in the Bible; it is "righteous", and "righteous" clearly means what Virgil meant.

I think "pious" came into use when "righteous" was discarded. "Righteous" belongs to fighting times of the Reformation, "pious" to that of secure Establishment. "Righteous" has an angry sound; "a righteous God" meant the angry Jehovah; and after the seventeenth century England was in revolt against the dominance of Old Testament ideas. Cromwell and Milton are great men, but uncomfortable companions, and I should think it very inapt use of language to speak of their piety. Indeed Milton was not addicted to the word, though it would have been enjoyable to hear his comment on Johnson's definition of a pious man as one "careful of the duties owed by created beings to God"; or on the Johnsonian saying which illustrates this so perfectly: "Campbell is a good man, a pious man, he never passes a church without pulling off his hat."

Many people in the eighteenth century would have thought this method of expressing piety Popish and un-English. But in essence Johnson is always typical of the English mind. Eighteenth century England agreed with him that piety was expressed in man's duty to God; and they all thought it pious to go to church. If you did not attend a place of worship—impious is a hard word, but at any rate you were not pious. And since it was generally held that morality for Christians must be based on revealed religion, the pious man was also logically the good man.

Yet the genius of the language never consented to identify goodness with piety. Piety was good, but not the whole of goodness; it was a specialised form of goodness. It was, moreover, suspect to the ordinary Englishman because it was closely associated with the observance of forms.

The translators of the Bible had failed to establish the word "righteous" in current speech; after the day of the Ironsides, probably no Englishman in ordinary speech ever said of another that he was a righteous man. But all through the eighteenth century, and for a good part of the nineteenth, "pious" was used quite naturally as a term of respectful praise. Yet I do not believe that anyone ever used it as he would have used "honest" or "kind". The word meant "religious", and rather more; one who was good because he was religious; and, since the Bible did not use it, there was always some hint of the new-fangled precisian.

Then there was the unfortunate association with the phrase "pious fraud" in which, if it be rightly understood, "fraud" does not mean a cheat, and "pious" certainly has no reference to churchgoing or chapelgoing. At all events, prejudice was created, partly by ignorance, partly by the cheapest form of jests.

It is a pity, for "pious" expressed to perfection a devoutness devoid of passion. It is a sober-suited word; there is something Quakerish about it. Friends of mine in the North of Ireland, Catholic peasants, are very simple, homely, quietgoing people, and the religion which penetrates their whole lives is strongly Puritan in its manifestations. Yet I could never fit the word "pious" to them. It applies perfectly to Protestant neighbours of theirs, living the same laborious lives on the same little holdings of unfruitful land,

98

yet living them under a wholly different inspiration.

And however the case stands with "pious", no one with a feeling for language will deny that "piety" is a beautiful and unspoilt word. No other conveys the same inflection of tenderness and reverence in the discharge of duty. Piety is neither austere nor threatening; it is exact but not severe. Why, then, is it that I, for instance, remembering my childhood and youth spent under the guidance of two people whose united lives were in their several ways a shining example of piety, cannot bring myself to speak of them as pious? Why is it that I, who can freely praise the memory of their kindness, their courage, their justice, their wisdom, and their sympathy, should yet feel reluctance to name what was, perhaps, the master quality in them both? Why should I avoid the word best fitted to sum up their virtues—their piety?

Many of us feel no more craving after piety in its normal sense than the tone-deaf feel for music, and the tone-deaf know they cannot praise music without impertinence. But it would be impertinence of a very different degree to undervalue the gift which one lacks.

99

If we are driven to admit that there is less old-fashioned piety in the civilised world than there used to be, we have also to recognise that no very satisfactory substitute has been discovered.

CHANGE

THEY say it is good to go away for a change, and so I went, to a country far unlike indeed the town where my abode was: to fields and waters so peaceful that the sound of a revolver was unknown. Yet that change had little interest or significance, more than the difference of decent days in the almanac from those when you have a cold in your head. If change was present to my thoughts, besetting me, jogging my elbow at sudden moments, much more deeply affecting and penetrating my whole consciousness, it was because I had come back to the places that I remembered in boyhood, half a century ago.

Change! In my boyhood, those to whom we belonged, those who were in Society's sense our "neighbours", owned and ruled that countryside. This twenty years and more, their power has gone, their ownership has been divided or has passed away: but to-day their successors, if they have successors, sit precariously in their homes, doubtful whether law will protect them in their tenure of what is left. Hardly anywhere in the world could change be completer. Yet the coachman who met me at the station—for in this household the motor-car had not made itself master— was the same friendly face that I had known any time these forty years. If he was changed, I, changing along with him, had never perceived it: and the house, when we drove up, was, as always, square, sunny, rose-and-creeper-covered, sitting pleasantly on the ground, as if it were a natural growth: the sweep at the hall door was covered with the same soft delightful shell-gravel that I could remember since I remember anything: for of all the houses that stand to-day this is the one that I have known longest.

The hostess who greeted me had not belonged to the place by birth, and of those who were born there, all had disappeared, some by the changes of living, some by that other transformation: and so, naturally, our talk was of change, and sad enough. Yet this elderly kinswoman of mine is of all my life-long friends the least altered. She had never seemed to me very young—perhaps because she was always looking after other people;

and now age did not mark her. Kindness and
cheerfulness defy time; and there is a quick-
ness of movement natural to the naturally
helpful on which years put little trammel.
In another house, with other hospitality, I
might not have found myself asking what
change, after all, had half a century made in
the country I knew best.

For, when I woke in the morning and
looked out on trees, they were the same trees,
their shape, their grouping, not altered. They
had grown, no doubt, but all the change I
could swear to was in the regiments of snow-
drops passing away, of daffodils marching
in, marshalled among their feet, my kinswoman's battalia. These were an innovation
of the last twenty or thirty years. But the
big central beech tree fitted exactly my earliest recollections: a fine tree in a fine group,
not towering, not conspicuous. It was otherwise down by the river where every bush
along the bank had been a feature and a
hazard for the young angler: and a great
straggling ash grew where I remembered a
sapling no taller than my trout rod. I did
not like that ash: it interferes with a good
cast, it is disorderly, ill-grown, and un-
tactful.

Still, looking over the country as a whole, where the two lives, man's and earth's, met and bred together, all transformation was for more strength, variety and beauty. If the big house was unchanged, the little houses were changed for the better; at the one I held in most affection, buildings stood where none were in my boyhood, a screen of trees that I saw planted now gave good shelter, and a patch of cold, barren moor had become wholesome garden ground. But the man who had accomplished this was beyond question old now, bent and shaken more than his years should warrant. A natural brain-worker and director of labour, his life had been squandered on the very hardest toil of back and limbs, tied to his few poor acres like a tethered beast; and the downward change in him was not compensated and retrieved by the upward thrust in those through whom succession should continue. Without the instinctive sense of that succession, life would be intolerable, we should all go melancholy mad.

For in that creation which we are pleased to call inanimate, in the world of earth-life with which we are in only partial communion, through which we trample as masters, doing our will, hacking, hewing, digging, ploughing, fertilising, destroying, disfiguring, beautifying, we count always upon one certainty: animation of the inanimate, the change that is renewal; and we are never deceived of our count. But in our own community, can we be so secure? In this excursion of mine, "for a change", I had run myself unthinkingly against the contemplation of changes which did not help to make holiday. The old order was changing, and I had belonged to the old order; something was perishing, and that thing was a ruling race. I remembered the old master of the house where I was staying —a noble in the strictest sense, who with perfect courtesy and composure would have held his own in any company or any council chamber; I remembered the refinement of his clean-cut beauty, the habit of command that underlay all his way of being, yet was never overbearing. He was the flower of his type, a type that grew out of conditions which change has abolished; I have seen the change, I shall see the type disappear where it lingers; and with it how much will be lost?

"Them that was rich, has nothing, them that had nothing has everything," said an old retainer to me, feeling, as retainers feel, the

change more acutely than those upon whom
it strikes directly. Yet during all these vicis-
situdes, in a country where nothing but
constant toil keeps rush and briar and heather
in check, no field that I know has gone back
into barrenness, and many an acre has been
won to fertility. Is the loss going to be
tragic? The only great and drastic change in
the human order of which Europe keeps
articulate memory was the French Revolution,
and how much after all did that affect the
human order in France? If we really knew
the answer to this question—as who, even in
France, really knows it?—many minds to-day
might be much more at ease.

For what matters, so long as change is
renewal? I found my heart suddenly rising
up in me at a house where the third generation that I had known was now in possession.
Age is shy with the young, a more painful
shyness than the young feel towards their
elders; and here I was a stranger, hardly a
memory, little more than a name. It was
good to be greeted by young, strong, active
people, and not greeted as a stranger: good
to meet new kindness in the old places: but
good above all to find that here, where
riches had stayed, there was a life far more

strenuous and laborious than ever the old order followed: a leadership no longer of command, but of example. Renewal, in short, and growth: a change which has abolished all touch of melancholy from my picture of the riverside which has always been my central image of the charm of running water. Yet if I came back happy from my holiday change, another and a simpler household has most to be thanked, for the sense that where my memory most instinctively returns, it can find other changes than those which sadden. Further up that same river is a lake, and heaven knows how many hours and days I have spent on it, and in most of them Hughie has been my boatman and companion. But I remember it before Hughie dipped an oar there; two squalid old brothers, drunken whenever chance offered, yet kind to my boyhood, were my earliest guides to those happy waters; and Hughie and his comrade John, who later replaced Micky and Charlie, were always boys in my notion of them. It was not altogether a welcome sign of change to find John bald and Hughie wrinkled as a March apple. Still, stray visits had made me aware of this process: but it was wholly a change to be welcomed this year by Hughies of a younger generation, issuing from the neat little cottage built where old Micky's hovel used to stand: healthy, hardy, redheaded youngsters, friendly as nice puppies—and passionate fishermen. For these many years I had been seeking a boy on whom to bestow half-worn tackle, doing by him as elder generations, to my great happiness, did by me. That search was ended; and I was a benefactor, secure of appreciation, as only those can be who give what costs them nothing. When Hughie and I have fished our last day together, other boatmen as keen and as companionable will be ready to take up his oars, and my name as well as his will be remembered, I think, for another fifty years beside Lough Fern.

When the ebb has begun in you, there is instinctive looking for signs of the flood making elsewhere. Humanity demands the double rhythm, the compensating movement, on which continuity depends. And according as your interest tends to fix itself more on life which is not your own, you are the more grateful to whatever and whoever in your downward motion will associate you with the rise.

It is possible, and it cannot be agreeable,

to come back to a town and find it changed out of recognition, out of your power to recognise it. This can never within a lifetime happen in a countryside where man merely works with nature and does not obliterate or cover up her features: and where you recognise every outline, the fields seem to know you, are the same, you feel unchanged. But in the human order a man may easily find that a society of which he was part has changed doubly out of recognition; he neither knows nor is known. Many of us in the war, coming back to a regimental mess after a year or even six months, had a furiously resentful sense of change. It is infinitely worse when your own country and your own people can no longer recognise you, and, as is natural, have no longer the desire to make that contact. Against this minor tragedy of change it is well to provide by keeping yourself articulately, and, if it may be, affectionately, in touch with some centre of renewed and recurring life in the places where you would not be forgotten. Human instincts will help you; if it is natural to drift apart, to grow apart, it is natural also that human beings should seek to maintain communication before they pass—on whatever road—com-

pletely out of hail. The wish to remember
is strong as the wish to be remembered; the
desire for continuity looks back as well as
forward, and I was as proud as a dog with
two tails because almost alone of those who
come to Lough Fern I could claim to have
fished with Micky, and kept in my retinue
of memories that brown shambling wraith.
Change has a pleasant rhythm when that
which is visibly passing is also visibly continuing, like the river at Hughie's door; and
the best of such an attachment as binds me
to those fields and waters is that each impression, which drives home the sense that
our day draws in, is compensated, muted and
softened by an increasing perception that all
we knew in youth survives in essence, is still
the same to us, and makes, though perhaps
with different accent, the same vague yet
beloved response to the same instinctive
movement of our love.

SPRING

SPRING comes singing. The birds are its interpreters, they waken the world to its own wonder: they are shouting to the sun before he swims coldly into the sky. In summer he will be a burden, heavy even on the birds; but after torpid winter he is light, he is warmth, he is life. Spring is life before life can be weariness.

Mortals, perhaps even all animals, are too gross; they have not faith sufficient to rise the heart in their clay with dawn, and till the sun is fully up they lie huddling. Very few of them really taste spring and its rapture. Sun for the herd means the sun of summer, scents for the herd are heady odours like the perfume of sweet peas. Yet it is in spring that the earth is truly fragrant; mixed with its breath is no exhalation of decay, such as summer must already master and overcome, and as autumn can only blend with its own essences. Spring smells of the sap, a faint yet clear message to our sense from the innumerable multitude of budding creatures; perceived as you smell the sea or the pinewoods, with the whole subconscious organism rather than in any definite moment, when you say, "It is here," and again, "It is gone." Yet when scarlet tassels drop from the balsam poplar you will catch it distinct as the waft from a beanfield; but unlike that cloying scent, it comes aromatic, pungent, tonic; clear, and sharp as the wind of dawn.

Yet when spring's message by the poplar gum reaches this distinctness to the sense, it is already past needing or heeding, for the leaf is there, visible in golden green, glossy with sap we smell. Spring's essential exhalation comes earlier, not from the leaf displayed, but from what has yet to unfurl. All the new year is there indeed, but tightly packed, under seal, covered and protected with its envelopes: the guest arrives, shy and unfamiliar, in travelling dress, all her gay costumes folded in her baggage: it is the birds who recognise and bid her welcome— the birds, and certain hearts, so quick in their leap of recognition that in spring they fore-run summer, as with the earliest notes of autumn they, like the birds, are clouded with the premonitions of decay. They, too, like the birds, are at their wildest when the rest of us shiver and incline to ask if it is not better indoors than out. They love the world best before it is bedizened: when the shape of trees, the springing rhythm of their growth, is visible to the last fingertip, yet when, for those who can see, all to the last fingertip is moving with the thrust of life; when contours of the bud are rounding, when the legion of hidden greennesses can be guessed in a mist of purple against the sky. Your extreme votaries of spring will hardly concede to April an equal charm with March; not even though in April all the form of trunk and branches may be divined through transparent apparelling of leafage and of blossom. Thrush and blackbird are more to them than cuckoo and nightingale: it is only the weaker brethren who wait to worship spring till spring comes like an army with banners.

And even then, what proportion of the world goes out to worship? Our usages in this world of European usage, no matter on which side of the Atlantic, tell of our indifference. We wait till after midsummer to make our holiday, we prolong it into autumn; town-dwellers hardly have sight or scent or sound of the year's freshness; they take no part in the earth's holiday, its high ceremonial. Yet the town gardens are there to give us notice: for the year's festival comes when the fruit trees are in blossom.

Beautiful an apple tree is when the fruit nestles and clusters red or golden among rough green leaves; beautiful a pear tree is when pears, glossy with a brown that shades to purple, hang among leaves glossy with purple and gold; but this beauty of fruitfulness is of the thing accomplished; work ended, it comes soberly and majestically home. Spring is wild, singing and dancing.

A painter saw in a little suburban garden a little pear tree, orderly and pruned to a pyramid; but the sun of April had played on it for a week, and every twig was in blossom. It stood there, fixed and rigid, tranquil and discreet to the gardener's eye; but the painter saw it otherwise and painted a lyric of spring. Nothing but whiteness was in the tree's picture, whiteness outlined in blue shadow; and about it and around it was sunlight, not as a gardener would have seen, but as the tree felt it; sunlight so golden that a tree must spend its last penny of life to make festival array. Many asked what the picture represented, for the cone of flowering boughs was broken and divided by the shadow in such a way that the design took a swinging rhythm as if the tree whirled on its stem. Painters are bad at explaining their vision in words: since they have made their poem, why should they try to make it again? But this painter afterwards was consoled by the observation of a Chinese writer, that an artist's business is not to paint a pear tree: it is to paint the dance of the soul of a pear tree.

Artists, in whatever kind, are the eyes and ears of us; they keep in their senses some of the primitive keenness, they see and hear what escapes the common world: and in this gift, which it is their task to maintain and augment, lies their real reward: it is worth more by far than the royalties we pay to some and the respect we show to others. Yet it is well to realise why and for what we others pay, if we do pay, homage or recompense. As these sensitives by their nature thrill to spring's first intimations, as the air is quick to them while for us it is still dead winter, so they have, in some faculty that lies deeper than sense, a realisation of spring's meaning which without them might be lost to half of civilised mankind. The labourer on the land, the labourer on the sea whatever his capacity—blue water sailor,

longshore fisherman, shepherd, cottier, or
director of the most modern farm—none of
these can need to be told that the earth has
its recurrences; these necessarily observe
"God's bright and intricate device of days
and seasons". But other millions of us, shut
in houses and streets of houses, working, if
not underground in mines, then almost
equally buried aboveground in some factory,
bank, shop, or newspaper office—what do we
feel or know about spring? And still the link
of contact is there, if we take care to be
aware of it; if even once a day we put our
noses out of doors, there sways before us
some trailing skirt of the pageant which pivots
on spring. Wherever we are, if our awareness be maintained, we can have our part in
the miracle when it comes; till it comes, we
can be made to feel that it will come again,
and—this is what the artists do for us—that
when it does come, it will be a miracle.

Artists are brought into the world to pro-
claim that the little brown onion buried in
the ground is going to be a daffodil. Skies
may be grey and lugubrious, the year littered
with wreckage, no gloss left on flower or
leaf, the splendours of decay not yet developed;
a drab, doleful day of later middle age, griz-

zled and gaptoothed, without the tranquil beauty which rests on white hair and yellow foliage; adventure ended, the harvest declared but not yet safe home; nothing uncertain but how much malign fate or incompetent futility may destroy before it can be finally gathered, consumed and forgotten. On such a day, in such a mood, where should courage be found to go on, if there were no spring coming? Read your lyrics, look at your picture; the artists are there to tell that the juice of each sodden leaf is passing to feed unseen currents, already busy with the hidden bulb, caressing, cajoling, pressing it into activity, against the time when the urging of forces from below will be answered by spring's summons, calling leaf, spike, trumpet and corolla upward into its purged and dancing air.

Is it in autumn one should be writing of spring? Or is spring time youth's possession? Youth is spring, no more aware of spring than the daffodil: it has never felt the ebbing sap, and needs no comfort from the visible renewal. Of course, in its black moments youth plunges abysmally, because it has never had occasion to notice that the world con-

tinues to go round. Nature has not arranged
consolations for the young: they are provided
for, the life force fermenting in their veins
will suffice to carry them through; or if not,
nature has no indulgence for deficient vitality,
and they may wither as they will; they are
none of nature's care. If humanity in its
wisdom or its folly choose to cocker and
cosset them, the artists, mediating between
humanity and nature, may be called in to
assist; they may invite the young to enjoy
the rhythm of their own despair, the glory
of its blackness: since action and reaction are
equal, to contemplate the downward swing
is at least to measure from what height you
fell. Useless to talk to the young about anything but themselves: youth must be in the
play, part of the forces it contemplates,
whether for jubilation or despair. Spring to
youth cannot come as a spectacle; nature
says to youth, "Join in", and the artists, if
they are to serve youth, must echo nature.
But to age, nature says, every year more
clearly, "Observe and enjoy".

Or, am I wrong? After all how mighty
little one knows outside a single consciousness. But I am well acquainted with a man
who, for a matter of forty years or fifty, was

so busy living that he never noticed how
nature clears the stage to gain emphasis for
her first unmistakable heralds of the spring.
Here in these northern lands, the hardest,
toughest, and most untractable are chosen
for the challenge; furze and blackthorn, able
to fight their way through anything. But
is there in all the year so delicate a whiteness,
so fairy-like an elegance, as the blackthorn
blossom, which—if you defy augury—will
flower in your vase for a score of days? Or
is there such another yellow, even in the
daffodil companies, as a whinbush puts on
in March? Yet of course in these latitudes
wild nature's first intimations are temperate
and reticent; the coltsfoot spike, the furring
of the willow, the tiny celandine. Only in
the garden, where we have borrowed from
the south, brilliances leap at us, alien to
these skies: crocus, more like a jewel than a
flower, blue of gentian, the exotic flame of
hyacinth or tulip. In spring each of their
comings is an event; it is not as in summer,
when you become aware some day that
Canterbury bells have been a week in bloom,
beside iris spikes that are overblown and
growing unsightly. In spring, nothing cum-
bers the ground.

Why recall what everybody knows who is
capable of sympathising? Only to illustrate
what it means to be reminded and made to
feel that all will recur: that for me who write,
as for you who read, there will come again
the sense of renewal, all the more welcome
the less of spring is in our stiffening joints
and in the jaded complex of our brain. The
year to-day may be spent and worn, it must
soon be dead and buried, we shall walk to
its funeral: but when the catkin is on the
sallies, salmon will be coming up from the
sea, strong, silvery, leaping embodiments of
spring, and some lucky day, some lucky
throw may bring one to our line.

But it will not be in Synnott's stream,
Michael, and you will not be there. It is
with the old friends in the old places that I
would worship the new year; and spring in
the world may bring doleful confirmation of
autumn in our lives. Yet if eyes and ears and
every sense are kept attentive, and attuned
by artists to the pageant and its music, we,
though we be little more than lookers-on,
may yet be partakers in the mystery of earth's
quickening—celebrants in our own place, at
our own pace, in our own fashion, of the
festival of spring.

ON BEING SHOCKED

THE young, on the whole, are considerate, and let their elders down easily. They select with reasonable care the pieces at the theatre to which they wish to take their mothers, their fathers, their aunts or their uncles. It is a question whether a mother is considered to be, on the average, more or less shockable than a father; and no doubt in practice the personal equation of each individual parent is classified and allowed for by the arbiters of what the elder generation shall be permitted to know.

But probably, as a rule, the mother is the parent who has to act as a buffer and protect the sensibilities of the elder male. She has had naturally a closer contact with the source of shocks; it is the daughter to-day who does the administering of them.

The whole male sex is still aghast at the spectacle of woman ranging loose. Men liked to regulate the dose for themselves. They enjoyed being shocked, have always enjoyed it since the time of Aristophanes—for that matter, in all probability from the first syllable of unrecorded time; and they have always been shocked about women; though by what precise trait in woman's conduct, varied with latitude, longitude, and the lapse of centuries. Essentially, however, men settled what should shock. The shocking was what shocked men. Women took the cue and were, as was expected of them, more shocked than their masters. It would have been shocking had they not been.

Nowadays woman settles all that for herself; and perhaps for the first time in human history man is more shocked than he likes to be. He is forced to think seriously, and no one likes to think under compulsion. The shocked male has to begin to ask himself, not whether it is shocking that a young woman should read, say, Paul Morand, but whether it is shocking that he himself should do so. He must either contract greatly the limits of his shockability or give them an extension which it will be inconvenient, if not impossible, to maintain.

What, after all, is the shocking? Certainly not the immoral. There was nothing immoral in articulating some of the many excellent

Anglo-Saxon words, mostly monosyllables, which usage discouraged or prohibited. Yet, even still the elegantly nurtured female can startle with certain nouns, and she is reaching out after adjectives which were exclusively a masculine prerogative; in short, she is treading on the heels of the cultured male who came back from the trenches with a mouthful of words and oaths, not exactly strange, but unfamiliar in their new atmosphere.

The desire to shock must be one of the ultimate constituents in human nature. Nobody is so refined, so genteel, so nice in thought and language, as to escape the temptation. A Victorian lady, by speaking of "a row", could achieve just as exquisite unfitness as her pretty granddaughter attains with "bloody". But woman is in charge now, and she, not man, will decide what is proper, what improper to be spoken, or spoken of. Even in ordinary friendship the young woman will now talk to the older man, as the young man, to his very great advantage, has in all periods sometimes talked to the older woman; and for this novelty the world has probably reason to be thankful.

Nobody is likely to deny that things need

readjustment, or that balance has been shaken. War, which abolishes the sanctions of certain original sanctities, shakes, if it does not remove, so many others, that we have no right to be surprised if there is a general lessening of fastidiousness. Allowances have to be made, and not for the young only, but for a whole generation. But it is well not to forget that society or a person no longer able to be shocked has lost in this fastidiousness a quality which is akin to honour—an instinct guiding conduct and judgment to avoidance, just as surely as honour prompts to action.

GRACE AFTER GOOD WORDS

A CRITIC is never so well employed as in giving honest thanks. It is in all senses a rare happiness, choice in quality, seldom found, when this emotion is created by a new author or a new work. Yet thanksgiving for what is new cannot have the confidence of final probation. The new dazzles a little, bewilders; and there is an inward monitor advising us against the temptation which lies in the delight of discovery. Besides, what will last in prose or verse can never be fully enjoyed, much less fully appreciated, at the first encounter. Our real debt is to the literature that we re-read; and time must elapse, the reader must change with time, before there can be absolute assurance that what appealed so strongly did not appeal to a passing mood.

I pay my thanks to-day, render my homage with assurance, and with the more cordial happiness because an old loyalty is in question. Many of us who learnt our trade of writing during the ten or fifteen years in which

Robert Louis Stevenson, still living, was famous, chose him for our master and champion. There was that in the known circumstances of his life and fate which commanded devotion as well as discipleship; perhaps not least of all, the knowledge which no one possessed so fully as he of his limited achievement. His craftsmanship stood admitted, but hardly one individual masterpiece, except perhaps that strange *tour de force*, "Jekyll and Hyde"; we certainly could not point to the well-nourished body of genial creative work which assures survival. While he lived, we his adherents were determined that he should be great, that he should survive, because of an allegiance which he had won, because of our attachment to his personality. I am sure that even when writing as a critic of the work of near friends I have never written so little dispassionately, never been so much an advocate rather than a judge, as when dealing with the art of this stranger, entirely unseen and unknown. It is almost twenty-six years since a detailed study of his novels by me appeared, in a review sufficiently important to make the publication an event for the young writer that I was then; but my chief satisfaction was a hope that pleasure and possibly even encouragement might come to this exiled chief of my craft, so far away in Samoa. Ten days after the review appeared came the news of his death; and the very real grief I felt had a quality which, as I now look back, seems significant. I grieved, naturally and instinctively, over the loss of what yet lay in him to do.

That, if you come to think, was an act of faith strangely mixed with doubt. It is scarcely possible that any writer's death should trouble any reader with a sense that the world is impoverished by it; our common store is already too inexhaustible. Grief was for the man's sake, not the world's; for a cherished career broken before it was secure of full and final development. To-day I find happiness in perceiving that the grief sprang from an error. The essence of this man lay not in his art but in his personality; and that personality is transmitted in a form certain to endure.

Exactly how much of Stevenson's work will continue to be read—except by the few curious—is of course highly debatable; and if he does not survive by his prose, whether in fiction or in the varying forms of the essay which he handled, then as an artist he has

failed. For prose was his special craft, on
which indeed he left a mark that no historian
of literature can ignore. But, speaking now
of survival in no such academic sense, I could
to-day more easily indicate pages in his prose
which have gone dead than those where
lasting life makes itself indisputably felt.
This negative attitude of mine, however, re-
presents probably some temperamental dull-
ness; what stands out vividly to my mind
to-day is the assured preservation of his
personality through a different craft. Stevenson, like so many others from Scott to
Kipling, was of those ambidextrous talents
which can use prose or verse at will—or
rather, as something which it is not their
will directs. In such a case, for what is
quintessential in the man, look to his verses;
they are nearly always written on an impulse,
for the sheer pleasure of writing. Nothing is
more characteristic of Scott, nothing expresses
Scott better, than his ballad of "Bonny Dun-
dee", born in the very hour when he bent
his great shoulders with a clearly settled
resolution to the task of clearing away that
mountainous debt. "Can't say what made me
take a frisk so uncommon of late years as to
write verses of free-will. I suppose the same

impulse which makes birds sing when the storm has blown over": so Scott noted in his Diary, private receptacle for so much, the like of which Stevenson habitually confided to the world. A writer of conscious self-study, of deliberate self-revelation, Stevenson has fixed the significant details of his life in admirable pages; and perhaps the assistance so given to our imaginations was the necessary condition for giving effect to his personality—which, as I insist, meant more to his generation and even to his disciples than his craftsmanship. Yet the survival of that personality, the force it still is, was revealed to me by no page of his prose essays, though to them I have turned back more than once of late. Nowhere did he give me that quickening sense of confirmation concerning a work's vitality which a critic cannot mistake. This final assurance I have in these days received from his verses, not indeed from his verse at large, but from a small group of poems, which are among the most truly autobiographic things in literature.

In quest of something to read to an invalid, for whom nothing in literature was too good, yet who had an invalid's craving for something that exhilarates, I picked up the "Songs of Travel", and on the way to the hospital looked into them. The poems were utterly familiar to me; in stanza after stanza, once the start given, I could have finished it from memory; yet with the open page came the direct voice, the contact with a living creature. There are times when any honest man in any country of Europe, and certainly in my own Ireland, may feel himself weighed down with a morbid depression; and I was sick of that disease, when suddenly it was as if clear sun and wind had chased the vapours off one. Well might the poet say:

> Bright is the ring of words
> When the right voice rings them;
> Fair the fall of songs
> When the singer sings them.
> Still they are carolled and said—
> On wings they are carried—
> When the singer is dead
> And the maker buried.

What first caught me was the gallant lilt of those lyrics that have roaming youth's desire for their burden:

> Give to me the life I love,
> Let the lave go by me,
> Give the jolly heaven above
> And the byway nigh me.

Or, better still:

> The untented Kosmos my abode,
> I pass, a wilful stranger,
> My mistress still the open road
> And the bright eyes of danger.

When the love-note comes into them, it has the same tone; the same personality breathes through it:

I will make my kitchen and you shall keep your
    room
Where white flows the river and bright blows
    the broom,
And you shall wash your linen and keep your
    body white
In rainfall at morning and dewfall at night.

These have the authentic voice of youth, but of youth with all youth's gravity as well as youth's light foot. It is the youth of a personality which out of its maturer mind inevitably frames a youthful vision of life's end. As I read these earlier lines, there ran, like an undersong in my memory, the "Epitaph" with its lovely close, soothing yet quickening, like rest in the open air:

> Here he lies where he fain would be;
> Home is the seaman, home from the sea,
> And the hunter is home from the hill.

Yet if all life be travel, travel is only one phase of life; and the "Songs of Travel" hold a complete revelation of Stevenson's personality because they show you also the traveller's heart when it is least content with its journeying. One felt always in him, beyond the gallant eagerness to see and know, to move instead of mouldering, a yet more gallant resolution to go on. This aspect of him could never be rendered in anything so simply lyrical as the few songs which I have named, or as the even more perfect "Sing me a song of a lad that is gone", where the melancholy of retrospect on youth's clean rapture is simple as the rapture it recalls. The heart of a man whom the zest of life has forsaken, and whom age has not yet tranquillized, is shown in a poem of very different order: I quote only the last lines of "If this was Faith":

To go on for ever, and fail, and go on again,
And be mauled to the earth and arise,
And contend for the shade of a word and a thing
    not seen with the eyes,
With the half of a broken hope for a pillow at
    night
That somehow the right is the right
And the smooth shall bloom from the rough;
Lord, if that were enough?

Who that has passed middle age, and tried to do anything worth doing, does not feel an echo to those words? Who but those who never really knew what was worth doing, or the very few who in their achievement found content? This is the natural cry of life's strenuous traveller, as the others are the songs of life's adventure; and together they give you Stevenson and give him you alive. No more is needed to preserve his personality; yet I would add to my group the lines written from Samoa in reply to the dedication of a Scottish novel by Mr. Crockett; probably also a stanza here and there from less completely successful poems, and certainly one isolated quatrain—"I have trod the upward and the downward slope". This gathering will complete for any sympathetic reader the human contact with him who died a generation ago, and yet this week was able to move and rouse me as no living friend could do. For what is imperishable in his poetry, I would add only the haunting verses to the tune of "Wandering Willie":

Home no more home to me, whither shall I wander?

and that, after all, is another phase of the

wanderer's mood, charged with Stevenson's personal colour. The single poem of his likely to matter to posterity, which may not be regarded almost as the direct expression of his own life, is that superb thing, "Mater Triumphans"; and it has far more affinity with his best prose than with any of his poetry, except what are really essays in verse.

For whereas in prose he was among the most complex and laborious of artists, his best verse is simple as some old ballad. It makes no pretence to technical mastery; and no one will claim for its author by reason of it a place among the great masters. I claim for him only that by it he lives not less assuredly than Lovelace by his lines to Lucasta, or Graham of Gartmore by his "If doughty deeds my lady please", and lives indeed more than they, with a fuller revelation of his being, a comrade giving counsel as well as comfort, source of strength as of delight. I know, having returned to it; and if grace after meat and drink, so easily come by, be fitting, then why not grace after good words?

THE HABIT OF BEAUTY

BEAUTY, like charm, does not come merely by nature; it is more than a lucky disposition of limb and feature; like the singer's art, it grows out of a natural gift and the desire to use it. This desire every singer has by instinct, and every beautiful person.

Only in use beauty is made perfect, and many are born with a physical endowment which they lack the genius to develop. Vulgarity or stupidity may disgrace the finest body and features. For beauty, when we speak of man or woman, means something different from the beauty of a landscape, a flower or an animal; it is a result, like a work of art; it is accomplishment; and for the height of accomplishment it depends on the conception of beauty which is in the mind of its possessor.

Beauty is the wrong word to use of a child's loveliness which, except for the promise, and also indeed, for the early promptings of nature, is no more than a kitten's. It has charm and delight. But beauty has power. Just as the singer or the poet is his own first and most essential audience, the beautiful person knows and sees, sub-consciously, how she looks or moves.

For beauty has not come to be beauty until it is aware of itself; its very essence is in bestowal; and the gift must have been recognised by its possessor before it comes to full flower in the graciousness of giving.

Where beauty is, whether in woman or in man, its power is felt almost equally by men and by women. The nun in a convent school may get as much worship as any of her sisters in the world, and may bestow her beauty as graciously; and the beautiful woman in the world gives instinctively to young and old, man and woman, with no more desire to trouble or subjugate than the artist feels in his creation. She obeys what has come to be the law of her being, and moves to an unheard music.

One must phrase it of the woman, for an ancient Puritanism inhibits. The Greeks were perhaps the last in Europe who could think equally of man and woman when they thought of beauty.

Sex appeal can never be extinguished. While the facts of life remain there will always be allurement in beauty: bird and flower, if they do not shape and colour themselves, are shaped and coloured to attract. But beauty in the true sense, though lying open to desire, is not provocative. That challenge destroys the repose and the dignity which in noble beauty are self-protecting. Beauty is neither warded in the home nor circumscribed by family circles; it is as general as the sun, but like the sun it can "purge the air of pestilence".

Who other than Shakespeare can render beauty? Homer, when he called up Helen, walking on the walls of Troy, and the old men, whose roof-trees were to burn for her, saying that it was no wonder men should make ten years' war for such a woman? Dante also, no doubt. Of prose makers, Fielding, Thackeray and Dickens never reach beyond prettiness. But there is one master here; Meredith conveyed again and again through his printed page the actual thrill of beauty. Yet indeed so also did John Galsworthy with his Irene swaying like an aspen under the airs of a sunny day.

The painters, of course, have done it—it is

their special privilege; and the one artist—Gainsborough—had the power at times to show beauty emanating from plain features.

For beauty may pass and kindle, suffuse or glow, momentarily, anywhere, and genius can catch and fix such moments. Yet to say that a human being has beauty means, properly speaking, something at command, no less constant than an artist's skill; it is a habit—literally, something that has become part of the nature by usage, and, metaphorically, a vesture which envelops and expresses the personality within.

People talk—people award beauty prizes—as if beauty were a matter of the face only. But beauty as an attribute of man or woman is harmony, and it is gesture, play of feature and of limb; a beautiful woman is beautiful in her downsitting and her uprising, in her way of walking and her way of talking; and though extreme youth has its bloom, and its natural suppleness of movement, yet the art of beauty is not completed till it governs every motion and makes every fibre eloquent.

When to that art once mastered is added the graciousness of a generous and lovely nature shining through, a beauty has been created which defies decay. For when the magic resides not in any flush of youth or transient moulding of the flesh which time can alter, but in the structure of the bones, the shape and set and line of the head and neck and figure, and when these are crowned by beauty of countenance, time may change, but can never disparage; a person so gifted, so accomplished, retains the accomplishment and the irradiation while life lasts.

HOSPITALITY

HOSPITALITY is always believed to be the special virtue of uncivilised countries; and in a sense that is true. I was brought up where the nearest hotel was a long day's journey through the wilds on whose outskirts we lived, and strangers used to arrive with some vague introduction, to be entertained and passed on. Consequently I have all my life been asking of more civilised people, as a matter of course, what very probably they would not have asked from me. Hospitality as we practised it in Donegal is no more than human decency; but the practice of it does tend to develop virtue; the one who feels bound to give what it would be churlish to refuse, soon takes a pleasure in giving. I learnt the pith of it from an Irishwoman in our midlands: "Put plenty of praties in the pot, Maria, you wouldn't know who would be stepping in to us across the bog." This was taking thought so that the stray guest should not only feel that he was welcome:

he was to see that his coming made no inconvenience.

I think that the "big houses" also, when they had to exercise a sort of obligatory hospitality, found their own ways of turning the obligation into a grace. After all, a change of company is welcome, and in outlying places every newcomer is a bringer of news. It is the height of hospitality to make your visitor feel himself good company, and I have known minds so hospitable that they could extract entertainment out of a statistician. (It is curious how often obligatory guests are dealers in, and seekers after, statistics: travelling M.P.s, or missionaries.)

Nowadays, what with the spread of hotels and motor-cars, the well-to-do are greatly relieved from obligation to casual hospitality. But in outlying places, it remains for the poor: and they take a pride in it. Very seldom you will go into an Irish cottage and not be asked to "sit down and take a cup of tea". "Grand strong tea they give you in Connemara", a district nurse told me; "you could trot a mouse on it." Even in households where other standards of excellence in tea prevail, it is hard to stop an Irish domestic from doubling the teaspoonfuls when a visitor is expected—

to show that there is nothing mean about the house. But also, I think, out of a traditional desire that any guest shall have the best that can be given. That instinct goes deep.

In our troubled times, a friend of mine was living in a lonely house among hills which had become a stronghold of the "Irregulars". One winter day the man whose name was a terror there came to say that the house must be burnt down. She faced him and turned him from his purpose; perfect courtesy and courage in a highbred woman are hard to resist. Some time afterwards, a score or so of his partisans descended on the house demanding food. That was a different matter; she did her best for them. As they departed, noticing one slip something out of sight, she picked up the saucer and found a half crown. There had to be pursuit and explanation that the household could not accept payment. "Sure," said the lad apologetically, "we did not want you to have your trouble for nothing." I am sure that those who offered a token payment for what they had needed were glad to feel themselves accepted as guests.

Still, in the ordinary relations of our civilised world, hospitality means something different from providing what is needed—food or lodging. It has to do with the pleasant extras—life's adornment: and it shows itself by taking thought how to give pleasure. Like all other virtues, it passes into an instinct, and the only thing considered is what will be the pleasantest way to do a pleasant thing. Brillat Savarin has an aphorism that when you invite a guest, you make yourself responsible for his happiness while he is with you. That may be true, but it is not good to dwell on it: there would be much less hospitality in the world if all conceived of it as carrying a responsibility. One knows indeed hard-working hosts and hostesses who cannot hide from themselves, or from their guests, how hard they are working; but these are exceptions and one is sorry for them—and anxious not to inflict such trouble again: just as one instinctively plans to come back to a room or a house where a welcome seems as natural as breathing. The sense of effort may set up a claim on the guest's gratitude, but it kills pleasure.

But what heroines some hostesses are! On them weighs the possibility of what may happen if guests come late: yet they will face

their company serene and smiling—unless
things go badly wrong indeed, and then the
wisest will take everybody into their confidence and laugh together over the misadven-
ture. For, after all, hospitality is not giving,
it is sharing; and some friends will feel
themselves privileged to take a bit of your
disappointment; it may be all the better party
because the soup was spoilt.

The hostess with whom I have often been
inclined to sympathise is one with whom
everything has gone too triumphantly right.
People have been so happily busy talking that
they have eaten and drunk without noticing
the array of carefully thought out elegances—
or if they have noticed, they have been too
English to refer to this fact. She and her cook
may next day exchange the expression of their
satisfaction; but she should have tributes to
pass on to the kitchen.

One lovely hospitality is the hospitality of
gardens. Miss Ruth Draper has been more
than usually merciless in her observation of
the garden hostess; but the kind of woman
whom she presents with those deft touches
is the kind whose flower beds you look at
from a distance. The hospitable gardener's
greatest delight in a garden is the privilege

of giving away flowers. Plants to those who have a garden of their own; but flowers, armfuls of flowers, to the town dweller. My mind keeps the enchanting vision of a beautiful young woman lavishly gathering through the garden she had made; delighting in the lavishness that could be shown without wrecking, delighting in the richness of the armful that she gathered, delighting because those who had shared with her the pleasures of her garden would be able to carry back more than a memory of it.

In an English home where I went often and was pampered in many ways, the height of hospitality seemed to me to lie in their provision of flat paper containers which could open up into receptacles, some of them big as portmanteaux; and in these the week-end guests carried back sheaves of tulips and narcissus, branches of rhododendrons, a whole pageant of the month. One almost came to feel a partnership in the place.

In the most perfectly satisfying hospitality there is always this suggestion of permanence. The French do not easily admit to their houses; but once admitted, it seems established that you are expected to come back. In England invitations are more casu-

ally given; the first in a way comes as a trial;
closer relations only come slowly. But how
pleasant it is to know a house where you can
count on feeling generally welcome; where
no company will ever be better than that of
your host, or your hostess, or both together,
over a cup of tea by the fire; yet where, if
it is question of lunch or dinner, you will
surely meet people worth meeting—pleasant
if they are a new experience, pleasanter still
if they are a pleasure renewed; but in any
case you will be in company assorted with
the same instinct as inspires a well-chosen
menu.

Pleasant also to go where your tastes are
remembered and consulted: I knew a cottage
where if I was expected there would always
be potato cake for auld lang syne. I knew a
poet's house where for another poet (now
famous) there would always be apple dump-
ling—or was it treacle roll? But most dis-
tinguished it is when other folk are drinking
champagne to be asked if you would not
prefer, it may be a senatorial burgundy, it
may be some claret miraculously preserved
from a vintage before the phylloxera—wines
that convey a perfume in the mention. Those
that have such treasures and take thought to

bestow them where they are appreciated "rightly do inherit heaven's graces"; they do not "husband nature's riches from expense", but share them out in a hospitality that offers a compliment as well as luxury. Yet after all the essence of that hospitality is neither in the luxury nor even in the compliment; it is in the kind thought.

WITHDRAWN

JUL 01 2024

DAVID O. McKAY LIBRARY
BYU-IDAHO